The Leopard

Gecko Advisor

A CUTTING-EDGE GUIDE TO THE PROPER CARE
AND HUSBANDRY OF THE FASTEST GROWING
PET IN POPULARITY IN THE WORLD

Ray Roehner

A Designer Geckos Publication®
SEDONA, ARIZONA

Designer Geckos
P.O. Box 2307
Sedona, Arizona 86339
www.designergeckos.com

All photos included in this book are from Designer Geckos' collection or are productions of Designer Geckos (and were taken by the author). Pictures may be used by permission only.

Front Cover photo: "Flame" - Tangerine White and Yellow Leopard Gecko.
Back Cover photo: "Mandarin" - Tangerine Leopard Gecko.
Both cover geckos produced at the Designer Geckos facility.
Cover design by Arnold Gonzalez.
Book design by Lucia Ashta.

The Leopard Gecko Advisor: A cutting-edge guide to the proper care and husbandry of the fastest growing pet in popularity in the world / Ray Roehner. — 1st ed.
ISBN 978-0-692-02627-4

Table of Contents

Acknowledgments

I'd like to express my deep appreciation to all the outstanding, dedicated people involved in the leopard gecko field that I have been so privileged to have been involved with in this exciting endeavor...to all the great breeders, collectors, and hobbyists that make this such an amazing journey. So many people helped to bring me to this point, that it would take a book itself to acknowledge them all. Many thanks to Ron Tremper, Steve Sykes, Garrick DeMeyer, and all the great gecko folks I have interacted with through the years as my passion and love for leopard geckos grew into this exciting chapter in my life.

The most influential and supportive of them all, my wife Carol, has really been the inspiration for me to carry on. Her love and dedication for geckos never ceases to amaze me. I recall one instance when I bought a $1200 gecko to add to our collection. When I told her about my order, she said, "Really? Great. What morph is it...do you have a pic?" I could see the excitement, and her trust of my judgment in her eyes. I knew from that point on that we would have success. She loves these animals as much as I do, and her tireless efforts inspire me every day.

I must also thank my high school Advanced Biology teacher, Ms. Louise Schwabe for her incredible inspiration, as well as rock musician Ian Anderson, who indirectly taught me to strive to have a strong work ethic and good moral character. And last but certainly not least, to my parents, who encouraged me to pursue my dreams, and allowed me to have a zoo full of reptiles and amphibians on our back porch throughout my childhood!

Ray and Carol Roehner – Cofounders of Designer Geckos®

Introduction

While many of you know who I am, many of you do not, so I thought it would be appropriate to tell a bit about myself. I started out pursuing my animal interests at the ripe old age of five. I would go on field trips by myself and with friends to try to encounter every critter I could find. I began my own collection, and our house was soon full of aquariums, terrariums, cages, and barrels full of my new little friends I'd find in my travels. I'd study them and release them, learning all I could about their biology, behavior, and husbandry.

I was very fortunate to be in the right place at the right time on several occasions, finding some very unique creatures on my field trips. I recall on one trip when I was about seven, while hunting for tiger salamanders. I overturned a large flat rock in a streambed and I was able to catch what could have been a record crayfish. This giant crustacean was bigger than many lobsters I had seen...just an enormous creature that I can recall to this day as if I had seen him yesterday. It was a wonder I'll never forget. I let him go, knowing that he was something very special that needed to be left where he was. The impact that finding him had on me was profound.

What really kicked off my reptile passion was an evening trip with some friends to a local field near a large freight train terminal in N.Y. There were six of us fearless youngsters, hunting for snakes at dusk in this large field, when we came upon a huge train door lying in the field along the tracks. We all grabbed an edge and flipped over the door. To our amazement, there were about 20 snakes of various kinds and sizes. It was a young boys' dream! We all reached down and picked up a snake. One of my friends picked up an enormous black snake, the likes of which none of us had ever seen before.

It was a massive animal, and very gentle and sweet. I immediately fell in love with this great reptile, and negotiated with him to do a trade with a nice milk snake I had caught. I named her Mother of the Mambas, Mamba for short. She was huge and very thick, solid grey-black, with a beautiful white belly. She quickly became my best friend and went everywhere with me. Everyone in my neighborhood knew her and we were inseparable. She was always around my neck.

Despite my fairly extensive knowledge at a young age, I was stumped as to what kind of snake she was, so one day my Dad took me and Mamba to the Buffalo Museum to meet with the curator. He examined her and smiled, and said that she was perhaps the largest garter snake ever found in captivity. I was incredulous and we left the museum, me doubting his conclusion that she was a garter snake. Then one warm summer morning when I went to get her out of her tub, there she was lying there intertwined with 33 beautiful little baby striped garter snakes! It was an experience of a lifetime for a budding young reptile enthusiast. Mamba changed my life, and I've been hooked on reptiles ever since. I miss her greatly to this day.

When in high school, I got my first job working at a cancer research hospital in Buffalo taking care of the research animals and assisting in the labs. That's where my technical background in animal husbandry began. From there I went on to college, working in labs developing experiments in bone marrow transplantation in mice. I went on to get a science degree as well as certification as an animal technologist.

My career then began working in pharmacology research for 2 major pharmaceutical companies for many years where I became an expert in animal research facilities, animal husbandry, cancer research management, regulations, preclinical drug development, research protocols, SOPs, and scientific methodologies. This career dovetailed very well with my love for animals, and it allowed me to continue being actively involved in the latest technologies, husbandry techniques, environmental aspects, research protocols, and procedures involving animals and research facilities.

I became very knowledgeable in marine aquaria then as well, and I had several marine tanks at home with some of the most amazing fish and invertebrates on the planet. But my real love for animals continued to be geared towards reptiles.

One day, while contemplating a lizard for a new terrarium setup in my office, I started to check into leopard geckos a bit more thoroughly, and was amazed by the exploding genetic aspects of the field. I decided to start an extensive collection, and the rest is history.

Carol and I had always wanted to do some sort of small business together, and producing leopard geckos seemed to be the perfect fit to meld my animal and science background with her extensive background in sales, marketing, and customer service. Designer Geckos was born, and soon after, we opened the first commercial storefront dedicated to leopard geckos in the world.

While we did not have aspirations to have a huge reptile operation and produce large numbers of geckos, we did want to strive to fine tune a leopard gecko care program that produced high quality animals in a humane way for the geckos, further the leopard gecko hobby, and foment ethical business practices based on top notch customer service for our fellow hobbyists. We had the goal of trying to make a positive educational contribution to the husbandry aspects of the hobby, seeing that there was really a lot of outdated, old-school and erroneous information both online and in other references on the market. We began to do extensive research within our own colony, developing procedures and methodologies that would have significant effects on the health and well-being of our animals. We took a very scientific approach to this effort, and made some very interesting findings as we went along. Our animals began to make their mark worldwide, and people wanted to know what we were doing that allowed us to produce the high quality animals that we were quickly becoming known for.

While many businesses may deem such knowledge as "trade secrets", we took a very altruistic approach to the growing requests from others to have us impart our knowledge. We knew that our research would not only benefit our customers and others in the gecko hobby, but most importantly, we might have a positive impact on the geckos that we so loved, in that they might have a better life if people around the world were armed with our methodologies. We began to give talks and disseminate our information to anyone who wished to have it. Education in leopard gecko care became a new calling for us. While we enjoyed this new aspect of teaching, we weren't able to reach out to the numbers of people we knew needed our assistance. Many asked us to write a book on the subject...and here we are.

I hope you enjoy this reference, and that you find it to be a useful adjunct to your current gecko care program. I have also included some bullet-point care outlines in the appendix of this book that you can photocopy and have handy for quick references, or to give to your friends to help them with their care program rather than having to peruse the book looking for a key passage.

While there are many care programs out there, and many knowledgeable breeders and collectors who use different methodologies that work well for them, we felt that our program offered something different and comprehensive that combined what was already in use and worked well, with our own ideas and procedures that we developed and had great success with. That synergy of ideas culminated in this book.

Our cutting edge care program based on our extensive research has worked very well for us, so we felt it was time for a new and somewhat different approach. The focus on this book will be on leopard gecko care and husbandry. I will not concentrate on in-depth biology or the myriad of morphs and genetics, as there are several good references already available on these topics.

Please note that I will also be making specific references to companies, vendors, and various supplies and products that we use in our program. This is not to make this book a commercial enterprise, but to provide you with the specific information on what we use in our program so you may use that information when selecting your own supplies and equipment for your gecko or breeding operation, whatever the scale.

Also note that proceeds from the sale of this book will go to various reptile causes, reptile rescue operations, and other animal welfare ventures...our way of saying thanks to the community and animals that have so enriched our lives.

Thank you for allowing me to convey my ideas to you. After all, this whole endeavor is for you...and the geckos.

Snow Diablo Blancos. This spectacular white morph, created originally by reptile breeder Garrick DeMeyer, is one of the most beautiful of all the leopard geckos. Unlike the Diablo Blancos that can sometimes have a yellowish cast, the addition of the Snow gene produces a very white gecko with virtually no yellow…truly stunning works of living art.

CHAPTER 1

Why a Leopard Gecko?

The leopard gecko is the fastest growing pet in popularity in the world today, and also has become the #1 reptile pet in the world. There are many reasons for the explosion in popularity of this wonderful little creature.

The following are some of the key attributes of the leopard gecko:

- *They are very friendly and easy to tame...they love people.* When describing leopard geckos to people who are considering them for a pet, I always liken them to a dog in a lizard's body!

Leos become very tame, each have their own personality and intelligence, they bond to humans very much like a dog does, and they can even learn to recognize certain words and phrases if you take the time to train them and socialize them. Now, I will say that geckos, like any other animal, have varying levels of intelligence and individualized personalities.

Some geckos are extremely intelligent and easy to train. I will get into this in more depth later in the book, but the key to human socialization of any animal is to get its trust. Once that is established, it's just a matter of spending quality time with the animal. The vast majority of geckos will become very tame if socialized properly. If your goal is to have a little couch buddy to watch TV with, or one to sit on your shoulder and go for a walk with, then it is best to get a younger gecko so it bonds to you at a younger age, as with a puppy. Once a gecko is mature, it may have established certain habits and a mind of its own, and it might be more challenging to re-train it. We generally recommend juvenile or sub-adult geckos if this is your goal. Having said that though, many people have great success acquiring mature geckos and retired breeders who make wonderful companion pets.

Geckos can live 10-15 years on average, with some living into their 20s, so please consider that obtaining a leopard gecko can be a long term relationship, and commitment. Be prepared for a long and happy life with your new family member, and please try to keep that longevity in mind so you never need to reach a point where a reptile rescue situation enters into that bond.

- *They are very clean animals, with virtually no odors, and can be paper trained.* Leopard geckos are little clean fanatics, and like having a very clean enclosure. We have found that geckos that are kept in clean conditions thrive, and respond with better growth, color, appetite, and tameness. My adult geckos that live at home often will tell me when they have just defecated by coming to the front of their terrarium or tub and even pawing to get my attention, as if to say, "Hey, I was busy in here and could you please get this out of here for me?"

I've seen this behavior pattern so often that I know that they are very clean animals and want to be kept clean. Additionally, geckos will choose one location in their enclosure for excretion, called a defecatorium. We use that behavior to our advantage in our terrariums by placing a small triangle of paper towel in their preferred corner.

They quickly learn to do their business on that corner of paper towel, which we just toss out and replace as needed. This low maintenance approach saves cleaning the substrate and terrarium regularly.

When I tell customers about this great new method we discovered, they look at me quizzically, but then they stop by or call a month later to tell me of their great success with this method. The lack of odors with leopard geckos is also a big plus. Many reptiles, especially snakes and large lizards, do have a noticeable odor. I can always tell when people have snakes in their homes when I walk in. With leopard geckos, you can have several in a room with no odor. I recall on many occasions that customers who visit our gecko store comment that there is no odor, when we actually have large numbers of geckos in the store.

- *They come in many beautiful colors and patterns.* Today's leopard geckos are indeed works of living art. The incredible explosion of colors and patterns have made leopard geckos some of the most beautiful animals in the world today. Hundreds of new morphs and crosses have become mainstream, and the geckos being produced today are truly stunning to see. Everyone has their own color, pattern, and morph preference, so there's a gecko out there to suit everyone's personal tastes.

Striped Zorro Bandit. "Lucky" is a direct offspring of Zorro. The Zorro Bandit line from Designer Geckos continues to be refined for boldness, markings, color, and temperament...truly a striking example of the types of amazing morphs that are created today by breeders worldwide. The Bandit is a beautiful morph discovered originally by pioneer reptile breeder Ron Tremper. Bandits retain their very bold markings into adulthood, and have a masked pattern or noseband as pictured here in Lucky.
They can come in striped, jungle, or albino form.

- *Leopard geckos are hypo-allergenic, the perfect pet for children and people with allergies.* Many children and adults as well have various pet allergies. Cats, dogs, birds, and rodents can be very allergenic, which prevents many people from having them for pets. Many doctors are now recommending reptile pets to their patients for this very reason, and in particular leopard geckos.

One thing worth mentioning, is that when handling any animal, regardless of species, it is good hygienic practice to wash your hands before and after handling animals, cleaning cages, handling feeder insects, etc. This is just good husbandry for the animals, and you. You can easily transmit a foreign bacteria to them which can cause skin or respiratory infections. More on these considerations will be discussed later in the book.

- *They can be left alone when you are away on vacation.* Going away for a long weekend is generally not a problem with leopard geckos. These creatures do very well in a solitary environment, and once adult, can go for considerable periods of time without food. If you are leaving for a few days, feed your gecko well leading up to your trip, and leave them extra water. While I generally do not endorse the use of humid hides (more on this later), vacation time is when you do want to use either a humid hide, or place a wet crumpled paper towel in each cave to assist in their shedding process just in case they shed while you are gone. When you return, check your gecko carefully and be sure there are no shed remnants on its toes or elsewhere. If there are bits of shed they need to be removed promptly. If you are going away for more than a few days, it would be a good idea to have a knowledgeable friend stop by to check the gecko to be sure all's OK.

- *Adults eat very little and are low maintenance.* Once your gecko is about one year of age, it is considered an adult. At this age, the majority of its growth is over and it will now just put on mass. I also instruct people to use the gecko's tail girth as the weight gauge. The gecko's tail should be in proportion to its body. While it is good to have some weight on the tail for a nutrient reserve, an obese tail is not healthy, and makes it more difficult for a gecko to maneuver and shed.

While hatchlings and juveniles need to eat every day due to their growth rate at that stage, an adult gecko can be fed much more sparingly. This makes adult geckos very easy to care for and maintain. Because they don't need to eat a lot, they don't defecate a lot either. This is one of the factors that makes leopard geckos one of the easiest animals there are to care for. While they may look up at you and act like they are starving, overfeeding any animal is never a good idea. Again, watch the tail to assess your feeding regimen and adjust your feeding accordingly. Remember that leos do not get a great deal of physical activity and thus don't burn a lot of calories, so their food requirements cannot be equated with that of other animals that are much more active.

- *They are nocturnal, sleep during the day, and ready to play at night.* An interesting facet of leopard geckos is that they are nocturnal. They generally sleep during the day, which works out well for us humans since we work or go to school during the day. Geckos become active around dusk and then are awake during the night. Nighttime is a good time to interact with your gecko, although they do fine being handled during the day as well.

The albino leopard geckos tend to be light sensitive, so if you want to handle an albino during the day it would be best to avoid brightly lit areas. Otherwise, leopard geckos are fine coming out to visit during the day. Whether day or night, leopard geckos will spend the majority of their time in their caves, as they do in nature.

- *They are inexpensive to feed and keep.* Leos are a very inexpensive animal to keep. Vet bills are almost nonexistent if you follow a good care program. We do not advocate the use of "hot lights", which we will get into in more depth later, so electric energy consumption is minimal. Leopard geckos are insectivores, and thus will only eat live insects. We generally recommend mealworms as the staple diet, and mealworms can be obtained from good sources in quantity at very low cost.

There are great insect vendors that you can buy from online that will ship your insect order right to your door. It can cost just a few dollars a month to feed a gecko, so this makes it a very affordable pet, compared to most other animals that can cost many dollars a month just to feed, not to mention vet bills, kennel costs, (or asking your neighbors to feed and let your dog out three times a day).

- *They are the perfect pet, a beautiful, happy little friend for all ages.* If leopard geckos are socialized properly, a very easy process, they quickly become a great companion animal and a friendly, lovable pet. Some geckos tame more easily than others, and they have variable levels of intelligence, which in many cases is dependent on the particular morph, as well as on parental intelligence.

Some are livelier than others, some more docile and laid back. Giants for instance, are genetically a docile morph, as are some of the designer morphs and

Mack Snows, among others. We will go into more detail on morphs in that particular chapter.

I have trained geckos to come when called, and to respond to various phrases, very much like a dog does. The term, "lizard brain" is a misnomer!

Many lizards, leopard geckos included, are actually quite intelligent, and have an intuitive intelligence much like horses and other species. Leopard geckos in the wild are prey animals, so they have evolved to be smart in order to survive.

I have seen geckos react in very remarkable ways that prove to me that they are very smart animals. They can also be trained to respect certain boundaries. Because they are very clean animals and very rarely ever defecate outside their terrariums, they can sit on the couch with you and watch TV, sit on your shoulder, etc.

Several of my collection males that live at home are so trained, that I can put one on a couch, leave to do something, and when I come back they will still be on the couch waiting for my return. I recall one day, I had one of my big males out on the couch with me, and I got called away to my store to meet with a customer who needed immediate attention. I forgot that Sunny was out with me! Then, after I finished my work at the store, I went to do some shopping. I came back four hours later. When I walked into the house and through the living room, there was Sunny sitting there on the couch looking up at me as if to say, "Forgot about me, eh?" He never left the couch. It was an amazing experience that further proved how incredibly smart these little lizards really are.

I spoke to one customer who has twelve leopard geckos, and he has a sort of family time ritual at night, when he gets out all twelve of his female geckos and they lie in bed each night and watch TV with him! Each one has its own preferred spot on the bed which they assume each night. One female goes into his pillow case, and turns around so just her head is poking out of the pillow case so she can watch TV while she is covered by the pillow case. She does this every night. This kind of behavior shows many things, but particularly the ability to think, reason, and have fun.

- *Males live 10-20 years, females 10-12 on average.* Obtaining a leopard gecko for a pet is not like getting a guppy or other short-lived pets. Geckos can live a long time with good care and have lifespans similar to a dog, so expect to have your little friend for many years.

 - *They can be taken anywhere when the weather is warm.* If trained properly, geckos can go most anywhere with you provided the temperature is adequate. I have gone for walks with a gecko on my shoulder quite often. Be careful that they are well trained for this shoulder technique so they don't fall off your shoulder, and always proceed with great care.

I've also found that trained geckos love to go for rides in the car, very much like dogs. They look around with amazement at the scenery, and seem to thoroughly enjoy the experience. I've taken geckos with me on my day job, where they spend the day with me in my office, meeting with my coworkers, and generally just having a great time.

I do things to enrich their life experiences because I like to see how their behavioral aspects can be developed. They never cease to amaze me. Geckos don't need to spend their lives in their terrarium. If you take the time and effort to work with them, you'll be amazed at just how special they really are.

Banded Lavender Giant. "Violet" is an amazing gecko, very intelligent, who loves to go for rides in the car. She is a great example of just how intelligent geckos are, and how tame and responsive they can become if you spend the time and effort with them.

CHAPTER 2

Responsibility

It's always perplexed me that there are pet shops and breeders that sell animals without having a thorough knowledge on their proper care to pass along to their customers. This lack of education not only does a disservice to the customers who may have a difficult experience because of it, but most importantly, it can have a very negative impact on the animals who rely on us for their care and well-being. That's one of the big reasons for this book. I hope to help educate those who sell geckos so that they become valuable mentors for their customers, and advocates and educators for the animals they produce and sell.

When buying a leopard gecko, it is also important to take the time and effort to find a knowledgeable reptile veterinarian in your area. While these animals normally require very little veterinary care, you should still be prepared for some unforeseen eventuality, which can come when you least expect it, and never at a good time. Finding a local vet that specializes in reptiles should be a high priority if you plan to get a gecko, or any reptile.

There are many excellent reptile rescue operations around the world that save, care for, and find homes for reptiles. It is also a good idea to find one in your area that provides excellent care and service, and help them with funding and assistance when you have the time and some extra money. I think reptile folks are among the finest people I've ever been associated with, and it's heartwarming to have witnessed the incredible dedication to reptile causes such as reptile rescues. Please try to donate and help them out when you can, maybe even volunteering. Many reptile rescue operations do not have enough funding to meet their needs, so we all need to try to keep that in mind and make an effort to help them out as highly valued members of our reptile community.

Having a leopard gecko for a pet is a long term relationship and commitment, and we always counsel people on that responsibility. It reminds me of people who buy a baby Macaw parrot, not knowing that the bird will be with them their entire lives, and likely outlive them...they can live to be 100!

While leos aren't around for that long, with proper care they can live for many years, and people need to be aware of that. I always think of the ethical and humane aspects of our hobby, yet many do not consider these types of implications when owning a reptile. It is wonderful to know that we will have our geckos in our lives for a long time, and we need to be sure that care considerations are #1, as they should be with any pet. We will have these wonderful little animals in our lives for many years, and we should prepare accordingly.

Another responsibility consideration is to try to help to educate others getting into the gecko hobby. The gecko community is a very tightly knit group of dedicated people who are always willing to impart their knowledge onto others. There are many great print references and online reptile forums, as well as social media and other resources. Do your part to further the hobby by helping others to learn all they can. We all benefit from this interaction, especially the geckos!

Attend reptile shows and seminars. They are always great learning experiences, and an excellent way to network and meet others who share your passion. Leopard geckos are the fastest growing pet in popularity in the world, so educating people is of paramount importance, and a responsibility we should all take an active role in. Remember, the only dumb question is the one you don't ask. Get involved, get educated, and become an educator.

Gecko Education. There is a wealth of information, both in print references, as well as online resources such as reptile forums. "Alfie" is showing us just how much fun the gecko hobby is.

CHAPTER 3

Choices, Basic Genetics, and Morphs

In recent years, there has been an explosion of new morphs and crosses in the leopard gecko field. This has created a tremendous variety for hobbyists to choose from, and this trend of new types of leopard geckos is going to continue. The genetics of leopard geckos is one of the most fascinating aspects of these animals, and is helping to fuel their massive increase in popularity. Geckos now come in an amazing array of colors, sizes, and patterns due to the industrious gecko collectors and breeders that continually search for new combinations and genetic variability to try to produce the new hot morph or cross.

While this exciting development has made the hobby even more interesting to be involved in, it has also resulted in a quandary of sorts for the hobbyists entering the field....so many choices! In the wild, leopard geckos are rather drab tans and browns so they can blend into their environment more easily. Now, the dazzling colors and patterns available in today's captive bred morphs is almost system overload for new folks getting into the hobby.

While color, size, pattern, eye color, etc. are all very important criteria for many when deciding what geckos to choose, there are two other factors that are perhaps even more important when choosing geckos. Personality and intelligence are now becoming big factors in the hobby, and some discerning collectors and breeders are now starting to realize the importance of these aspects.

Horse and dog people have long known how important the temperament and intelligence of the parents are when selecting their animals. Physical criteria like strength, size, body conformation, health issues like hip dysplasia in dogs, high-strung behavioral issues in horses, and other such factors are extremely important considerations when selecting a puppy or colt, and the parents are scrutinized since genetics play a considerable role in these attributes.

The same holds true with gecko personality and intelligence. "The apple doesn't fall far from the tree" is an old adage that is relevant in animals, and as it does in many species, geckos are no different. More and more consideration will be given to these factors as time goes on and people realize that intelligence and temperament matter in a gecko as well, particularly since it is an animal they will have for many years.

I have experimented with various breeding combinations to confirm this theory, and have been stunned by the findings. Our most intelligent and docile geckos with the best personalities produce offspring that are almost cookie cutter productions of the parents. I've witnessed very specific behavioral patterns in juvenile geckos that are so identical to the parents that it's uncanny. The same holds true with intelligence. Smart geckos produce smart babies. Geckos with strong appetites have offspring that have strong appetites. Picky eaters produce babies that are picky eaters. I've seen these types of things over and over again, which has lead me to this theory. I think as time goes on, more breeders will start to focus on those attributes. While many collectors and hobbyists have the main consideration and goal of specific phenotypes of color or markings, many will start to look for geckos that make good couch buddies as well. I predict this will be one of the next focus areas of gecko production for many in the future.

The physical appearance of offspring also can very closely match the parents. Zorro, the patriarch of the Zorro Bandit line developed by Designer Geckos, has a perfect number "3" on the left top side of his neck. His well-known daughter, Lucky, also has a perfect number "3" in the exact same spot on her neck. That's how specific and amazing gecko genetics can be. Two Bandits with full noseband markings on their faces will produce the majority of their offspring that will have the full noseband, a genetic trait that has amazing specificity. The male offspring of our Hot Moose Super Giant, Moosie, look almost identical to him in every way, with the same face, head, and body structure, as well as personality.

When selecting a gecko, it is important to choose a gecko from a reputable breeder that produces high quality, parasite-free geckos of known genetic background. The gecko should be active and healthy, not hyperactive, and the body should be free of malformations such as jaw misalignment, missing toes, kinked tail, and eye issues. While body malformations are not necessarily an issue for pet geckos, they can be issues if you plan to breed the gecko as some malformations can be genetic. The body should appear healthy with good skin integrity and appearance. The eyes should be clear, and the tail should be properly proportioned to the body. Never select a gecko with a thin tail as it could be a sign of parasite infection. The tail should have decent weight but should not appear obese or unusually large. Leopard geckos store fat reserves in their tails, and it is good to have some fat storage in the tail, but it should not be excessive.

Male and female leopard geckos are very docile, so it is a matter of preference whether you wish to acquire a male or female as a pet. Geckos can often be sexed at a young age. Males exhibit sex characteristics of perianal pores anterior to the vent, as well as a hemipenal bulge posterior to the vent. Male albinos can often be sexed as early as 10 grams in size, while some of the pigmented geckos like Bandits and Mack Snows may be more difficult to sex for the average hobbyists until they reach 20 grams or more.

Two or three females can generally coexist quite nicely in the same enclosure provided they have adequate room and hide space. It is important to monitor that they are all getting adequate food, as some females can be very aggressive eaters while others are more timid eaters. A male and female generally should not be housed together except at breeding time or the male can become quite aggressive at times, stressing the female. Two males should never be housed together, or even placed in proximity to each other on a couch, etc., or a fight will surely ensue!

In recent years, the internet, reference books, forums, expos, and journals such as *Reptiles* have provided a wealth of information on the care, breeding, and genetics of these amazing reptiles. That infusion of knowledge has created a community of experts that strive to further the leopard gecko hobby with their hard work and diligence in researching and developing new morphs and crosses in what is now an exploding new field in herpetology.

The sky is the limit when it comes to producing the various crosses being produced around the world today. Many breeders have their own lines of morphs, each with its own characteristics, colors, patterns, and sizes. True "new morphs" are more difficult to come by, with many so-called new morphs often times being variants or crosses of other existing morphs.

When selecting geckos for a breeding project, the breeder must have a solid plan in place to achieve the desired result, with thorough knowledge of the genetics involved. It is imperative that geckos are acquired for the project that have a known genetic background, which can be a challenge. Due to the explosion in breeding of leopard geckos, the gene pool has gotten somewhat questionable in recent years, so finding pure genetic animals has become more difficult. Many so-called pure genetic animals may have various heterozygous backgrounds often unbeknownst to the breeder until they start to produce animals and find odd results popping out of the eggs! Acquisitions must be done with this in mind, so new breeding projects can be established on a solid genetic footing. Obtaining breeding project geckos from reliable sources that can assure genetic integrity of the animals is imperative.

There is a lot to know about breeding leopard geckos when you take into account heterozygous, homozygous, dominant and recessive genes, etc., and anyone considering breeding projects should do their homework before embarking on a project. There are excellent genetic resources on the market, as well as websites, forums, and social media venues. There are also online genetic calculators to utilize that will give a fairly accurate prediction on breeding outcomes based on the genetics you plug into them. It is also a good idea to find breeders who have worked with similar projects to get their input. Most reptile breeders are very altruistic and willing to share their knowledge.

Leopard gecko genetics are very fascinating in many ways, and I am finding that not only are the genetic outcomes quite predictable, but that other traits aside from phenotype are also transmitted down to the offspring. Some geckos are more intelligent and social than others, some are better eaters than others, and various other traits like personality are very often genetically determined.

Genetics also play a role in the handling ability of morphs, and certain geckos are very mellow, while others are more lively and more for advanced hobbyists. I normally recommend the more docile morphs for children and beginners.

Some of the designer morphs such as Bandits and Mack Snows are quite docile, as are the Giants, which are genetically a very calm gecko. Giants are some of my favorite geckos for this reason. Super Giants can achieve sizes up to 12 inches in length, and though a larger gecko than your regular leopard gecko, they are easy to keep and make wonderful pets. The Giant genes are particularly exciting to work with. If a Super Giant is bred to a regular sized leopard gecko, roughly 100% of the offspring will be Giants. Super Giant x Super Giant produces 100% Super Giant offspring. I have found in my Giant projects that the offspring look and act almost identically to the parents, and particularly so with males looking and behaving like the fathers.

Line breeding (breeding morphs with similar traits to each other) is common in reptile breeding projects, and astute breeders select the best offspring examples for subsequent breedings so that each generation continues to be refined to produce higher level animals. For instance, in the leopard gecko community, there are many different lines of Tangerine leopard geckos, each having a slightly different coloration. Many breeders select the best Tangerines from various lines and combine them to refine and produce their own new line. The Designer Geckos line, called Mandarin Tangerines, is a refined line that combined the best examples of many different lines until we came up with the attributes we were looking for. Mandarins are known to have unique coloration and are a large, robust gecko. Many breeders are continuing to refine these various Tangerine lines to produce their own look.

We all remember the Punnett squares from Biology class, a simple chart method to determine breeding outcomes of known genetic backgrounds (genotype). The phenotype refers to the physical appearance (color, size, pattern, etc.) of the gecko. A homozygous gecko has a genetic background of two of the same gene alleles, and if the alleles are different (one dominant, one recessive), the gecko is considered heterozygous, carrying the recessive gene.

When breeding geckos that are heterozygous, both parents would need to be heterozygous for the same recessive allele for that particular trait to be expressed in the offspring.

Some traits are due to one gene that has been changed (single gene traits), while some are polygenic (influenced by multiple genes). Some of the more popular leopard gecko polygenic traits are Jungles, Stripes, Tangerines, and Bandits. Some dominant trait examples are White and Yellows, and Enigmas, and co-dominant examples (where both alleles are expressed) are Mack Snows and Giants. Recessive traits include the various Albinos, Blizzard, Patternless, and Eclipse.

The combinations and possibilities are endless! Leopard gecko genetics are complex and can take up a book full of information. Topics like test breeding, trait proving, mutations, and gene linkage are subjects for advanced genetics, and I encourage any serious hobbyist to do their due diligence if they endeavor to perform high quality breeding projects.

The genetic and breeding complexities are astounding, and since the reptile hobby has become so mainstream, my hope is that reptile genetics experts will consider offering classes and tutorials to assist hobbyists and further the growth of the reptile field and hobby.

I will not delve into a great deal of information on genetics in this particular book. There are already excellent references available by experts in the field, and there are genetic calculators online that will give you the breeding outcomes of the various morph combinations. The Holy Grail of course, is coming up with a new morph, but a true new morph is not easy to come by. The majority of so-called new morphs, are often crosses and combinations of existing morphs, however new variations are being discovered.

Mandarin Tangerine Enigma. This young female from the Mandarin Enigma line is a striking example of just how amazing some of the various crosses are. Leopard geckos go through various pattern and color changes as they mature from hatchlings to adults. This gecko will look very different when it is mature than it does in this juvenile picture.

Here is a list of some of the widely-held morphs and their attributes:

- *Giants and Super Giants.* When a newbie first hears the term Giant, they think that it will be some sort of enormous animal that they maybe cannot handle. While Giants and Super Giants are a bit larger than a regular sized gecko, they are not enormous, and are very easy to handle. They are genetically a very tame morph, easy to keep, have wonderful temperaments, and can have high levels of intelligence. I have a Super Giant Sunglow that comes when I call him, and I have witnessed some amazing behavior from him. Giants are one of my favorite morphs for that reason. They make great companion geckos, and are actually quite easy to handle and care for.

While the majority of Giants and Super Giants are of the albino variety, many with white, yellows, and oranges the predominant colors, more morphs are starting to be genetically super-sized, a trend that will continue. While some may claim to have available geckos that are designated Giant or Super Giant, sometimes they are not. True Giants have a different head and body structure than a regular gecko that happens to be just a large gecko. Experienced hobbyists can tell by looking at a gecko if it is a true Giant based on its structure. I have a Tangerine male (Mandarin) that is 120 grams, but I do not consider him a Giant...he's just a very big gecko. While this may sound confusing, it really is pretty clear cut if you work with this morph a lot.

Tracking the genetic background of Giant and Super Giant offspring is generally quite accurate. For instance, if both parents are confirmed Super Giants, then close to 100% of the offspring will be Super Giants. Super Giant babies are usually longer at birth than a regular gecko, and have long whip tails and very long toes. By 2-3 months of age the tail gets very long and the body becomes quite elongated. They usually have voracious appetites at a very young age, and grow quickly. Females do not get nearly as large as the males, and though a genetically confirmed female Super Giant may not grow to be a very large gecko, she carries the SG gene and will produce SG babies if bred to an SG male. Male SGs can get as long as twelve inches in length and attain weights upwards of 170 grams.

My experience working with these has lead me to theorize that SGs that are power fed and grow to massive weights may have shortened life spans. It may be that while G and SG geckos evolved through selective breeding to be enormous in size, their organ systems may not necessarily have evolved in the same way, and can't handle the mass of the animal.

While this is only my theory, I have made the decision to keep my large male SGs in the 125-140 gram range. They seem to do very well at this size, and I haven't experienced any early mortality or illness issues.

As for size of enclosures for G and SG geckos, all geckos do very well in moderately sized habitats. We will get into this in more detail in the next chapter on setups. One thing I do with my larger geckos is to enlarge the opening of their caves so that they can go in and out easily. While an 11-12 inch Super Giant male may not be the best choice for a young child to handle, these gentle giants are wonderful geckos and should be considered to be one of the best pet geckos for someone who prefers a little larger gecko.

Super Giant Sunglow. "Ronnie" is a stunning example of an albino Super Giant. He is an extremely intelligent, massive gecko, with brilliant golden coloration and a lot of carrot tail, which is rather unusual in the Super Giant lines.
He is my most prized gecko in our collection.

- *Bandits*. These beautifully marked geckos are favorites in the gecko world. They most often make an easy gecko to handle, and a nice low maintenance animal. They are generally moderately sized geckos, often have good intelligence levels, and are usually a reasonably priced animal.

This is a good choice for someone looking for a nice gecko that will be easy to care for, and is in a reasonable price range.

The Bandits are a striking designer morph, often with very bold markings that they retain through adulthood. Bandits all have some sort of mask marking on their nose, with the most sought-after having a full noseband marking across the bridge of the nose. Bandits are a thick bodied animal, and they are usually very good shedders and eaters. They have become one of the most desirable morphs worldwide. Bandits are smart and personable geckos, and easy to care for, making them one of the best choices for someone looking for a nicely marked gecko. Bandits are one of the few morphs that look basically the same when hatchlings as they do when adult as far as their markings. Many other morphs go through considerable color and pattern changes from hatchling to adult.

Bandit. "Zorro"...our book would not be complete if we didn't have a picture of Zorro in it. This world-renowned gecko has produced some of the most spectacular, bold Bandits in the world, and his offspring are highly sought after. He is not only a beautiful gecko, but is very smart with a great personality. Note the full mask/noseband and very jet black bold markings...truly a beautiful morph.

- *Tangerines*. One of the most popular morphs worldwide is the Tangerine leopard gecko, with one of the most commonly produced being the SHTCTB (Super Hypo Tangerine Carrot Tail Baldy). There are many different lines of Tangerines today, with each breeder seemingly having their own line. The Tangerine is a beautiful gecko with adults having a golden orange to rust orange coloration and varying amounts of orange carrot tail. When hatchlings, Tangerines generally don't look like a particularly impressive morph, but they quickly attain dazzling color, and when they are around 5 months of age, their orange coloration and carrot tail are usually quite stunning. As they mature, as with many morphs, their colors become more subdued, but they remain a very attractive gecko. Tangerines are usually excellent eaters and shedders, and are easy to maintain, making them an excellent choice for a pet gecko. Male Tangerines can be somewhat more lively, and females are often very mellow and easy to handle.

Tangerine (SHTCTB). "Jason" is a truly stunning gecko, with amazing orange coloration and an incredible amount of bright orange carrot tail. From the original Gecko Genetics line of breeder Jason Haygood, this outstanding gecko has great body structure, and is the father of Mandarin, the foundation male for the Designer Geckos "Mandarin Tangerine line" (see back cover).

- *White and Yellows.* The White and Yellow (WY) morph is a genetic variation discovered in Belarus in 1996. It is a beautiful gecko, with unique coloration and bright white sides and belly. It is known to be somewhat of a morph
enhancer (similar to the Enigma), and is now widely used in various crosses to
produce unusually colored geckos. Tangerine White and Yellows are among
the most colorful of the WY morphs, and many breeders are now working on
various WY projects to see what other variations and crosses might be good
additions for the leopard gecko community. WYs are a smart and friendly
morph, and can be somewhat of a discerning eater. While in the past, WYs
were mainly geckos for the high end collector, the gecko has become more
mainstream as more breeders produce them for the market and prices have
moderated. It is important to obtain true WYs from the original strain, as many
WYs on the market today may not necessarily be from this original strain.

Tangerine White and Yellow. Designer Geckos' WY, "Mars", is perhaps one of the most
beautiful and highly-valued geckos in the world today. From the Tangerine WY G Project line of breeder Matt Baronak, this gorgeous gecko has nice bright coloration and a
very unique red paradox spot. Note the bright white sides, typical of this morph.

Tangerine. Shown here as an offspring example of a "Mars" WY crossed to a Sunglow female, you can see how beautifully the Tangerine gene was expressed in this stunning gecko. This is the reason that WYs are being used in various combinations to produce new crosses.

- *Mack Snows*. One of the most popular leopard gecko morphs is the Mack Snow. Mack Snows are widely available at reptile shows and pet shops at reasonable prices, and they are probably the most popular of the morphs among beginner hobbyists. Known for varying shares of lavender, light gold, and black markings, often greatly spotted, this easy to keep morph is generally very docile, and a good eater and shedder. Mack Snows are used in various crosses, and are a fun, low maintenance gecko.

Super Giant Mack Snow. "Buffalo Bill" is a legendary Mack Snow that is the foundation male for the Designer Geckos Mack Snow line. (Mack Snows are known to be a very docile, easy animals to handle, and are a Favorite among young hobbyists.)

- *Enigmas.* Perhaps the most intriguing of all the morphs is the Enigma. Enigmas are very beautiful and unique leopard geckos that can have very wild markings and colors. Many breeders have worked with Enigmas with varying degrees of success due to the unfortunate neurological defects genetically inherent in this morph. Many Enigmas have various defects that can cause them to spin, star gaze, and move erratically, and some even have problems eating. Because it is such a beautiful morph, many breeders have endeavored to breed out the neurological defects, often times however with no success. This is not a beginner's morph and is best left in the hands of experienced gecko collectors until it is further refined. I have been working with Enigmas crossing them with the very robust Mandarin Tangerine line, and thus far I am very encouraged by the results and have found very few neurological issues in any offspring to date. I believe that if Enigmas are crossed to very strong morphs, that the defects can be diluted to the point where they are virtually nonexistent. Time will tell on this, however there is the hope that this morph can be salvaged so that it is able to live a normal life and interact as a regular gecko, and still provide the benefits of its outstanding beauty.

Mandarin Tangerine Enigma. The Enigmas are stunning geckos that can have amazing colors, markings, and patterns. Because of the occasional neurological problems of this morph, they have not become mainstream, however great progress has been made in recent years in the refinement of those issues, so there is hope that this beautiful morph will one day soon overcome past difficulties.

- *Designers.* "Designer" is a somewhat generic term interpreted in different ways, but basically it is often a combination or cross of various morphs, and some examples are Bolds, Stripes, and other forms that have attractive colors and markings. Designers are generally pigmented, but there are albino types as well. Bandits can also be considered Designers. Due to a form of hybrid vigor, Designers are usually a very hardy, robust morph, and they are generally a very low maintenance gecko that sheds and eats well. Designers come in many varieties, and they make a good choice for either beginners or collectors.

Zorro Mandarin Designer. This beautiful juvenile Designer was produced by Designer Geckos and is a combination of the best examples of the Zorro Bandit line and the Mandarin Tangerine line. Each subsequent generation will continue to improve in colors and markings, making this a very desirable Designer leopard gecko.

- Snow Diablo Blancos. While not a common morph, I felt that it would be worthwhile to discuss some of the white morphs that are very popular with some hobbyists. White geckos such as the Blazing Blizzard, Diablo Blanco, and Snow Diablo Blanco are very striking geckos to see in person. The Blazing Blizzard has both the Blizzard and Albino recessive genes. It can have variable eye color, and often has some very slight hues of gray to yellow. The Diablo Blanco has red or snake eyes, and is also very white, often with a slight yellowish cast on its back.

The ultimate white gecko is the Snow Diablo Blanco, which is the Diablo Blanco with the Snow gene added. It is almost a solid pure white gecko with red eyes, very stunning to see in person. All of these white geckos are somewhat lively morphs, and not for beginner hobbyists. They are generally very good eaters, very strong, robust geckos, but they are very difficult to assess as to when they are ready to shed because of course, they are white. Unless you are a very experienced gecko keeper and check your gecko daily, the white morphs should have a moist hide in their enclosures to be sure they do not shed when you are away for a period of time and get stuck shed remnants on their toes and elsewhere. (More on Shedding in that chapter.) When a white gecko has shed it is imperative to check the gecko carefully in good light and remove any shed remnants promptly.

Snow Diablo Blanco. "Earl the Pearl" is quite a specimen...pure white with solid red eyes,
he is really a sight to behold in person, almost like porcelain in appearance. He is a
strong animal with a ravenous appetite, and a friendly albeit lively personality. These
are another great example of just how far the leopard gecko
genetics have evolved in recent years.

- *Eye Color.* A great deal of interest has come about in recent years on the various types of eyes and eye color in leopard geckos. From the red eyes of Raptors and other morphs, to black eyes of Eclipse types, and on and on, this new aspect is garnering a lot of attention. Here are just a few examples of some eye variations:

Buffalo Bill. This amazing Mack Snow Super Giant exhibits spectacular eyes... silver with maroon veining.

Mandarin Tangerine Enigma. The beautiful dark brown eyes of this Mandarin Enigma are really a sight to behold in person.

Marble Eyed Sunglow. A great deal of interest has grown in various marble eye types…
a very beautiful and unique eye color variation.

Bandit. This beautiful Bandit has a more typical eye, although many Designers have varying eye color.

We could go on and on about the myriad of different morphs being produced these days, and new morphs and crosses are being introduced regularly. There are experts in the genetics field who have written books and contributed a wealth of information online about this fascinating subject. I tried to touch on a few of them here just as examples, but I encourage people getting into the hobby to delve into this incredible topic of leopard gecko genetics. While many are just looking for a nice pet gecko, it is often an evolving process that drives them to look into the genetic aspects a little further. Few animals in the world have the genetic wonderment that you'll find with leopard geckos...truly an animal like none other.

Mandarin. "Manny" shown here bathed in sunlight in an outdoor setting, is a great example of just how beautiful leos are.

CHAPTER 4

The Setup

L eopard geckos are very easy to care for, and their habitat requirements are really simple compared to many other species. There is a wide array of options, and leos are not particularly fussy about how you house them, as long as they have the essentials, which we will get into in these next chapters.

There are many excellent terrariums on the market today that will work very well. Aquariums will also suffice, though not quite as ideal as terrariums made for small reptiles. A 20 gallon aquarium would be the minimum size, because you will need enough floor space for two suitable caves (hides), and dishes for water, supplements, and mealworms/food.

Conversely, large aquariums and terrariums are not particularly suitable for a leopard gecko, unless you are going to have a colony of geckos. Leopard geckos instinctively are prey animals, and they are very wary of the possibility of a bird or snake lurking around in their environment. A smaller setup allows them to know every square inch of their enclosure and gives them a much more secure feeling that will help them to thrive.

Many new hobbyists often ask me what my thoughts are on putting a leo in a large 55 or 75 gallon aquarium, and I always discourage that for these reasons. One customer set up a 75 gallon aquarium in a very elaborate and beautiful way, with many caves and structures to try to make a very naturalistic environment despite my advice. A month later he returned to tell me his gecko was very afraid, didn't want to be handled, wouldn't come out of its cave, and wouldn't eat. After I again discussed the setup issue, he put the gecko into a smaller setup and it did very well from that point on.

Since we are all animal lovers, we feel a need to provide a spectacular environment and feed them constantly, thinking we are neglectful guardians if we do not. But we need to think more like a gecko, in that they want to feel secure and unthreatened in a safe home. Leopard geckos in the wild stay very close to their rock crevice and don't venture far away, waiting for a bug to crawl by their opening.

Even in rack systems, it's amazing how large geckos can thrive in a relatively small 15 quart tub. So please take these things into account when choosing a habitat for your gecko. It'll be happy you thought like a gecko.

I have tried various setups to try to determine the best choice for a leopard gecko application. I will go into detail on our chosen terrarium setup as well as supplies and accessories in this book, not to endorse a particular company, but because we have found that certain items have worked very well for us. There are many great companies that produce a wide variety of equipment and supplies that are likely just as good as what we use, and our mentions of specific items in this book in no way are meant to diminish the other companies that also provide these items in the reptile field.

The terrarium kit that we generally recommend is 18x18x18 in size (see following photo and the Appendix for manufacturer info) and is ideal for leopard geckos in that it provides all the room for the required accessories and still gives the gecko a little room to roam without feeling threatened in an enclosure that is too large. While the 18 inch height is really not necessary, we've found that it is nice to have the additional height for working space for us humans when performing tasks inside the terrarium. It also provides for a decent amount of air space and stable ambient temperature comfort for the gecko when used in conjunction with our lighting, which we will discuss in that chapter. The kit we use comes with a few accessories that you will not use for leos, such as a bag of sand, temperature and humidity gauges, a large cactus, and a large rock structure...use those items in your garden. The other items in the kit will be used, and the kit sells for a reasonable price considering the quality of the terrarium and other included accessories you will use. It comes complete with a foam rock background, a full locking screen top (that's cat proof), dual locking front doors for ease of terrarium duties and gecko handling (also cat and toddler proof), a light hood, one cave, a nice water dish, and a small decorative cactus. The terrarium is well made, well designed, and of high quality construction.

So while you may pay a bit more than using an aquarium for your setup, keep in mind that this is an animal you will have in your life for many years, and having a nice setup for your gecko, and you, is really worth the investment. I've had hobbyists cost compare with all the accessories using an aquarium, and this kit only ends up costing a minimal amount more than a comparable aquarium set up the same way.

It is also a very aesthetically pleasing unit, and looks like a nice scenic setup even in a living room. We find this to be a great value and people who get this unit are always very happy with their decision.

Ultimately, it is the gecko we need to think about, and having the right amount of space for its needs, making it feel safe and secure, having a unit that is cost effective to operate, and providing a locked terrarium to preclude cat and kiddy mischief is worth it. As I said, there are many different types of units on the market, but be sure when making your habitat selection that you keep these criteria in mind.

Now, for the specifics of the setup...the terrarium itself comes fully assembled. You will not need the aforementioned items, the rock structure (they spend too much time in it and don't stay warm enough), the large cactus (takes up too much floor space for the other accessories you will need), the side wall temperature and humidity (not needed for our application), and the bag of sand (never use sand for leopard geckos!).

If you lay the terrarium unit on its side, you will apply an under tank heat pad in one of the bottom rear corners. Be sure you stick it onto the bottom glass of the terrarium precisely, because if you try to take it off you could damage the pad. We generally use the 30-40 gallon size under tank heat pad (UTH) for this particular terrarium. Smaller heat pads do not cover enough surface area to provide uniform heat under the warm cave. Once the heat pad is in place, turn the terrarium back upright, and carefully slide the background up and forward so it is away from the back glass. You will need to use a thermostat to regulate the temperature of the heat pad. There are reasonable on/off types of thermostats, that will keep your UTH temperature in the prescribed range of $89\text{-}93^0$F with good reliability. A good proportional thermostat is best but the cost may be prohibitive for many hobbyists. The less expensive on/off units work well for most terrarium applications.

Remove the screen top of the unit and drop the probe wire for the thermostat behind the background and out the bottom, pulling out about 4 inches of wire with the probe from the bottom of the background in the corner where the UTH was placed. You will also need a good quality thermometer with your unit to monitor the temperature of your UTH and surface under the warm cave. We recommend a good quality LED thermometer with probe. It is an inexpensive thermometer but really quite accurate (I've checked them with certified thermometers for accuracy).

Drop the probe wire from the thermometer behind the background and also pull out about 4 inches from the bottom of the background. Next, take the two probe wires from the thermostat and thermometer, run them alongside each other, and tape the probes flat and firmly with masking tape to the substrate (liner) centered over the UTH (which is placed on the underside of the bottom glass). Carefully slide the foam rock background back into place. This will make for a nice neat installation with no exposed wires.

For this setup we recommend reptile carpet as the substrate, specifically the 40-50 gallon size terrarium liner (size 36x18). It comes in a roll and you will have enough for two pieces, so you have one extra for a swap-out at cleaning time. Cut the liner precisely in half after measuring your terrarium floor dimensions. Reverse roll the carpet so it will lay flat on the bottom of the terrarium (you can also iron it with a warm iron to get it nice and flat if you wish). Lift the background slightly out of position so you can tuck the back edge of the carpet under the background to make a nice neat installation. The carpet can be vacuumed as needed to remove calcium dust or shed particles, and also cleaned easily by taking them outside on a clean surface (like the hood of your car), and blasting them for a few minutes with the hose. Drip dry for 5 minutes and they are ready to be put back into the terrarium.

The next step is to run the other ends of the probe wires out the top of the unit slots and put the screen top back in position. Plug the UTH into the thermostat, and plug the thermostat into an electrical wall outlet. Place the light hood onto the top of the terrarium at the back of the unit. The LED thermometer will slide into the top slot of the light hood. Adjust the thermostat in very small increments until your UTH/warm hide surface temperature is staying in the 89-93 range on your thermometer. This may take a couple hours to get adjusted just right, but once adjusted and in the prescribed range, it will maintain that temperature without further adjustments.

Place a 15 watt red light bulb into the light hood. Only one bulb is usually needed, and it is for our nighttime viewing purposes only. Leave the 15 watt bulb on 24/7. It is only a night light and if left on will last for many months. It also provides a little ambient warmth to the terrarium, and a low wattage red bulb will not disrupt the nocturnal gecko's light cycle. Hot lights are not to be used with leopard geckos...more on that in the following chapters.

It is also a good idea to get a small piece of plexiglass cut to fit the top front area of the screen top. This will keep the ambient temperature more stable, prevent cold drafts into the unit, and reduce external noise. There will still be a slot across the back for airflow so your gecko will still get plenty of air exchange.

We're almost done. I can complete this entire setup in about 20 minutes, so it isn't as complicated as it might sound. Now, take the one cave that came with the kit and place it over the UTH area. That is your warm hide and that surface should be kept in the 89-93^{0}F range as stated. You will need a second cave for a cool hide. The kit cave is a medium size cave, so you'll need to get another one, and those are readily available at pet outlets and online. The cool cave will sit in the other corner opposite the warm hide and off the UTH area. Leopard geckos need to thermo-regulate their body temperatures and they will go from one cave to the other as they wish.

Place the small cactus and water dish along the front glass of the terrarium. You'll also need two small dishes, one for mealworms and one for your supplements. The final item is a Designer Geckos copyrighted idea (not really!). Cut a small triangle of paper towel, and place it in one of the back corners...this is the bathroom. Geckos learn to use the triangle of paper towel, which makes your job much easier. Just toss it out when used and put a new one in place. This method keeps the terrarium carpet clean, and you, and your fastidious gecko happy. It's amazing how they learn very quickly to do this. Leopard geckos are little clean fanatics, and once they learn your trick, they will use it every time. We have used this method with very large Super Giant geckos and it's incredible to watch how precisely they line themselves up so they can make their deposit precisely onto that little paper towel triangle!

Your setup is done. We will have this instruction sheet in the Appendix of this book so you can copy it as a reference while you are putting together your setup if you wish. No matter what setup you decide to use, please keep these basics in mind. It will make your life easier, your gecko experience even more enjoyable, require less maintenance, and will provide your gecko with the perfect habitat throughout its lifetime.

Terrarium Setup. Here's a floor picture of our recommended setup as described in this chapter. It is simple, secure, functional, and offers the gecko an excellent home for many years to come.

CHAPTER 5

Temperature

Now that you have your habitat in place and are ready for your gecko, we need to discuss the parameters for proper care. Again, these procedures in our care program are my preferred methods based on our extensive research. Others may have ideas that they prefer and that have worked well for them. The purpose of this book it to provide you with our methodologies so that you can make an informed choice as to how best to proceed with your own care program.

Temperature is a very big factor in reptile keeping, regardless of the species. All reptiles are of course cold-blooded, and need warmth to properly digest their food. I have done a great deal of work on all facets of temperature in relation to leopard geckos, including parameters in daily care of geckos, incubation temperatures, shipping temperatures, and ambient/room temperatures.

I've found in my studies that the ideal warm hide surface temperature is in the range of 89-93^{0}F. While many references prescribe a lower range, we have found that this slightly higher range is more conducive to better color, growth, appetite and even temperament. This range is particularly important when raising the various albino morphs in order to keep their colors bright. Albinos that are kept at a lower temperature range often turn a brownish color, particularly the tail, and their colors diminish considerably.

Other morphs as well are affected by lower warm hide temperatures. Tangerines for instance can get noticeably duller in color and turn a brownish orange if not consistently kept in this range. Even if cool for a short period of time, the color loss is often irreversible. While this doesn't affect the genetics and the ability to produce bright offspring, it has a marked effect on geckos subjected to lower temperatures.

Conversely, some gecko keepers think that more is better, and keep their geckos at much higher temperatures. This can have a very adverse effect on geckos, and can even cause organ damage and premature death if kept at high temperatures for prolonged periods. This could also have a negative effect on breeders and ovulating females.

In one study, I tried keeping warm hides at 95^0F and found the geckos constantly laying outside their hides...it was too warm for them and they made that quite obvious. I would caution those who keep their geckos in this warmer temperature range of 95^0 and above to reconsider this practice. In summary, my recommendation is 89-93^0, with 90-91^0 being the ideal warm hide surface temperatures. I also have found that night drops utilizing cooler temperature ranges during the night, while slightly reducing energy costs, has a noticeable effect on the geckos' colors and appetite. My recommendation is to use the 89-93^0F range 24/7.

Now, there is one time that cooler temperatures can be beneficial if you are not concerned about diminished color and appetite, and that is with brumation and cooling down breeding females and then raising the temperatures back up gradually to simulate springtime and bring on ovulation. This is an acceptable practice used by many breeders who wish to get a jump on the breeding season. The method we have used for this is again quite different than most, who often times use somewhat radical temperature reductions. I have found that by gradually lowering breeder rack temperatures to 80^0F for one month, and then gradually raising the temperature back to normal range is all that's needed to induce ovulation. Do not feed females during the cool down period as they may be unable to properly digest their food. I have known others who lower the temperatures down even into the 60s, but I've found that this isn't necessary and could even be harmful for the females' health.

As for ambient temperature, I've found that this is not as critical as the warm hide surface temperature. We certainly don't want the ambient temperature to be cold, but room temperature to 80^0 is fine. It is best to avoid drafty areas for your terrarium, and as stated, it is a good idea to cover the top of the terrarium to maintain a stable temperature environment, leaving a small space for air exchange. Reptile enclosures should never be placed in windows or areas where direct sunlight can overheat the unit.

The more consistent you can be in all environmental aspects, the healthier your gecko will be. All animals thrive in homeostatic conditions, so we should strive to keep their habitats as stable as possible for optimal health.

It is imperative that you use a thermostat in your setup, whether it be a terrarium or rack system. Under tank heat pads without thermostats to control them are extremely variable in temperature, and if plugged directly into a wall outlet, they can be anywhere from 80-120°F due to normal voltage fluctuations in many areas.

The best thermostats are the proportional type that maintain a steady current through the heating pad or heat tape and keep temperatures in a very stable range. I use proportional thermostats in all racks and terrariums and temperatures stay very stable, usually in a one degree range.

The extra cost is easily made up for by reduced energy costs, and healthier environments and animals. The downside is that these can be a bit more expensive than what a beginner hobbyist can initially afford on top of the other associated costs with getting started, so in that case I recommend a good on-off type thermostat. There are a few good ones on the market, and they are less expensive to be sure. Whatever your budget allows, please be sure to use a thermostat in your setup.

As for rack systems, a proportional thermostat is a must if you want to keep stable temperatures across a number of different shelves and many different tubs. The best way to accomplish this stability in temperature is by drilling a small hole in the back of the rack, midway up the rack. Run the probe for your thermostat through the hole, and place the probe directly on the heat tape, and tape it down securely with several pieces of masking tape so the probe is completely covered and immovable. Place the probe next to the center divider or at the outer edge of the rack tub slot so sliding the tubs in and out doesn't hit the probe, but so the tub can slide over against it. This is an important point for temperature stability and cannot be overstated. If the probe is not right up against the tub your temperatures will bounce all over the place. We mark the shelf that has the probe taped to the heat tape with a piece of tape which reminds us to be sure when we slide the tub into that slot to be sure the tub is pushed towards the center divider (or edge) so the tub rests directly against the thermostat probe.

Then, using a dummy tub setup with a cave and thermometer in place and moving it from slot to slot, determine what temperature your heat tape needs to be in order to achieve our 89-93°F range in every tub, top to bottom.

For instance, you may find that you need to set your digital thermostat temperature to 94°F in order for the internal tub surface temp under the cave to be 90-91°F. Make adjustments until your rack slots are consistently reading in that range. It's a bit of work to do this monitoring precisely, but once done, you shouldn't have to bother doing much with it again other than your periodic monitoring with your dummy tub. Temperature monitoring should be part of your daily gecko routine. Heat pads and thermostats, while extremely reliable, can occasionally fail. It is a good idea to train your friend who will check in on your gecko while you are away on vacation to know the proper temperature range and check it daily.

Also, it is good to use a quality backup thermometer to check your temperatures periodically so the temperature coincides with the readout you are getting on your thermostat or other thermometers. There are excellent thermometers with probes on the market for a very reasonable cost. I use a dummy setup to check all my racks routinely. This setup is put together just like any other tub in the rack, with a paper liner and cave. I place the probe of the thermometer in the dummy tub under the cave and tape it securely with a piece of masking tape to the paper liner under the cave. Then by inserting this tub randomly into other slots from rack to rack, I can be sure that our thermostats and heat systems are functioning properly and my temperatures are in our prescribed range. In a rack system, there is often some variability from top to bottom shelves, but it is generally only a degree or two. As an example, if your middle tub is set for 91°, the top shelf tubs might be 89° or 90° and bottom shelves might be 92° or 93°.

There will be some variability due to the construction of the rack, but as long as all tubs are in range it is fine. We use this to our advantage by placing albinos in the warmer tubs on the rack to keep their colors bright. At reptile shows, we often hear of people who are having trouble with their geckos not eating, getting thin, losing color, being skittish or lethargic, etc., and the first thing we ask is what do you do for temperature. Most times they look at us very quizzically, like, "what do you mean"? Then we go on to train them, often spending considerable time, because they were never properly educated on the proper care and setup parameters.

We also give educational handouts on leopard gecko care to hobbyists at shows to spread the word on proper care, and we encourage other breeders at shows to do the same. Leos are the fastest growing pet in popularity in the world as I've said, and we need to do our part to be sure the hobby is growing on a stable and secure foundation of training and education. We all benefit from this, especially the geckos that rely on us completely for proper care.

CHAPTER 6

Humidity and Shedding

N ow, as for humidity...this is a topic where I really deviate from the norm. Years ago, I did some thinking about leopard geckos and where they originated from, the very rugged and arid Middle East. I had long heard that humidity was an important aspect to leopard gecko care, and was puzzled by this since they are not a tropical species. I started to analyze the humidity factor in my care program, and after careful consideration coupled with my own testing, I came to the realization and conclusion that leopard geckos really didn't need humidity at all, except at shed time to facilitate the shedding process. My conclusion in fact showed that humidity could actually be detrimental in many ways to the well-being of leos.

There are many reasons for my premise. Not only do leopard geckos in the wild not have regular access to a humid environment, but the myriad of successful breeders in the world who house many thousands of geckos in rack systems, don't generally use humid hides in their tubs, and with great success. Humidity can actually cause disease, since warmth coupled with moisture fosters an ideal breeding ground for bacteria, which can lead to skin, mouth, eye, and respiratory infections.

I measured temperatures in various humid hide setups I studied and found that humid hides are generally considerably cooler than our prescribed temperature range. This leads to reduction in color, growth, and appetite, since humid hides are very comfy for geckos and they end up spending far too much time in them and not enough time in their warm hides. I saw greatly diminished color and appetite in conjunction with humid hide use, particularly in albinos and the Giant morphs.

The dilemma in this theory, is that leopard geckos actually do need humidity at shed time in order to have a successful shed and accomplish complete removal of all shed remnants, particularly on the face and toes. The vast majority of gecko keepers are very astute hobbyists and check their animals at least daily.

It is simple to predict when your gecko is about to go into a shed by the cloudy, milky appearance of the skin. Geckos will also exhibit unusual behavior the day prior to a shed by staying in their hides, even at feeding time, and they often will not eat the day before they shed. What I do at pre-shed time when I see geckos getting that cloudy appearance, is immediately take a half of paper towel, wet it thoroughly and crumple it in a ball and insert one in the corner of each hide. This produces a humid environment inside each hide, and allows the gecko to have a successful shed. In my racks, I take the wet crumpled half of paper towel and place it in a back corner of the tub over the heat tape. The tub becomes like a sauna, and the gecko sheds very easily.

Once the gecko has completed the shedding process (yes, they do eat their shed), you should take your gecko out into a well-lit location and examine it very carefully for shed remnants, paying very close attention to problematic areas like the face, eyes, vent, and especially the toes. If any specks of shed remain you must remove them promptly. A warm wet Q Tip works well for this, or a 5-10 minute soak in a dish of ½ - 1 inch of warm water makes this removal a simple task. If shed remnants remain on the toes, the shed remnant will quickly constrict the capillaries in the toe causing bleeding and loss of the toe, a permanent affliction.

Now, if you are not able to check your gecko at least once a day to ascertain if it will go into a shed, then a humid hide might be for you. Albino geckos and especially the white geckos, can be extremely difficult to predict when they will shed, so it may be prudent to use a humid hide in those enclosures to avoid stuck shed issues. But again, my recommendation is not to use them, unless you feel you really need to. My geckos thrive in dry conditions, and I never have infection issues to deal with. My geckos stay bright and have strong appetites and excellent growth rates, so I stand by my assertion that humid hides may not be necessary for most. Egg laying females on the other hand, do need some moisture in their lay boxes, whether using moss or coconut fiber. This is the primary reason why breeding females lose their color, but of course, moisture is necessary for the egg laying process, and this is one instance when moisture is warranted.

My goal is to try to do my part to educate as many as I can about all care aspects, including pet stores, breeders, and hobbyists, and that's why I decided to write this book. While keeping leopard geckos isn't rocket science, there are many things to know if you want to use cutting-edge techniques and have top notch, healthy geckos.

Lunar Eclipse (Super Snow Eclipse Fasciolatus). These beautiful geckos, a production of breeder Michelle Gianvecchio, are an example of a very light animal that may be a candidate for periodic use of a humid hide unless you are a skilled gecko keeper and can recognize the onset of shed time. Upon completion of the shed cycle, geckos must be checked very thoroughly for shed remnants, which should be removed promptly.

CHAPTER 7

Lighting, Cleaning, Substrate, and Accessories

I do *not* advocate the use of hot lights for leopard geckos. This is one of the most common issues we hear from people who have bought their setup and gecko from pet stores who sell them hot lights for their terrarium, with negative health consequences on the geckos. Of course, overhead lighting is required for many reptile species, but certainly not for leopard geckos, a nocturnal species.

In our terrarium setups, we do use a 15 watt red bulb for our viewing purposes. This red light does not significantly affect the light cycle of the geckos, it affords viewing light at nighttime, and produces some ambient warmth for the enclosure. We recommend that these low wattage nightlight bulbs be left on 24/7 so the ambient warmth is consistent, plus the bulbs last much longer then if they are turned on and off daily.

People have discussed this point with me, stating that the stores and references they have checked out recommend lighting. I explain why hot lights are not warranted with leos, and also explain that the majority of our geckos live in rack systems with no lighting, and they are all extremely healthy. My adult males are massive and super healthy, and are some of the biggest geckos in the world, and they never get lighting other than handling in ambient lighting and an occasional hike down the road on my shoulder. Proper vitamin and mineral supplementation is crucial and that will be discussed in the next chapter.

Also, heat rocks should never be used for leopard geckos as they can overheat and burn the delicate skin of leos.

As for substrate choices, in rack systems, paper towels are the norm. Some use no substrate in their rack tubs, but paper liners of some sort should be used so the animal isn't sliding around on the floor surface, which is hard on their joints and particularly problematic with young geckos whose bones and joints are in the formative stages of growth.

We use laboratory grade paper liners cut to our tub specifications so change out is a very simple process. Leopard geckos are very clean animals and respond to high quality care and a clean environment.

When changing out paper liners, you should wipe out the inside of the tub with a disinfectant to kill possible bacteria, mold, and fungus. Many use chlorhexidine solution, which is an industry standard used as a germicidal agent in many vet clinics and animal facilities. It does have an odor, and is not effective on spores, so my preference is a good quality quaternary ammonium product diluted to specifications. I have used Quatricide PV15 for many years with excellent results and no adverse effects in the animals (1 tablespoon per gallon of water, dispense in spray bottles...label the stock solution clearly). I worked in the cancer research field for many years, and we used Quatricide as a germicidal disinfectant in working with immune compromised mice that were very fragile, with no adverse effects, so I had complete confidence that it would be effective in geckos. The other benefit of this product is that it has zero resistance issues, so it can be used for years without bacteria building up resistance to it. It is a very effective agent, and has no odor. Just spray a small amount of the diluted solution onto a paper towel and wipe out the enclosure. Wipe out thoroughly to remove all residual amounts of quat, but rinsing is not necessary. A microscopic layer of quat residue forms an effective antimicrobial barrier when dry. The only species that it should not be used in is cats. Cats are sensitive to quarternary ammonium and can get mouth ulcers from contact with quat residue. Otherwise, it is a very safe product and will keep your enclosures clean and free from pathogenic organisms.

I do not recommend bleach solution for enclosure cleaning due to the somewhat toxic chlorine fumes, particularly with pregnant females and young geckos. (Additionally, never expose leopard geckos to toxic fumes such as strong cleaning solutions, deodorizers, paint or solvent fumes, or any compound with a strong chemical odor. These fumes can have disastrous effects on geckos and other reptiles and amphibians.)

Sand should not be used as a substrate for leopard geckos. While it looks nice and naturalistic, the chance of intestinal impaction is too risky and potentially fatal. It is also hard to keep a terrarium with sand clean. Other substrate choices are tile, slate, and our preference in our terrariums, reptile carpet. We do not free feed our geckos so they do not get their teeth caught in the carpet, which is always a common concern of hobbyists when we recommend carpet.

All of our geckos are either fed mealworms in a dish, or are carefully tong fed, which I will explain in the Feeding chapter to follow. I think sometimes it is important to try to think like a gecko, so I tell people to ask themselves, if you were living in a terrarium for 10 years or more, would you rather live on a hard surface like slate, or a soft surface like carpet?

The other discovery we made, is that by placing a small triangle of paper towel in one of the back corners of the terrarium carpet floor, the geckos quickly learn to use the triangle for their bathroom. Then you simply toss it out and put a new triangle in place. That keeps the carpet clean, and maintenance simple. If you have a larger terrarium with multiple geckos, take ½ of a paper towel and fold it lengthwise and place it along the back or a side of the terrarium and all the geckos will learn to use this "runway" for their bathroom. It's amazing what little clean fanatics these geckos are and how quickly they learn to use the paper towel restroom!

The geckos will occasionally walk through their supplements, or have some bits of shed on the floor, and this can easily be vacuumed up as needed. When you want to clean the carpet, simply remove it from the terrarium, take it outside and blast it with the hose for a couple minutes (first use a soap solution or quat if needed), drip dry, and replace.

We have been using reptile carpet for years and find it to be our substrate of choice for terrariums.

As for other accessories, we use medium size caves in all enclosures. They are well made and the perfect size for leos, as well as very washable. We use a small grinding stone on a drill to smooth edges of the cave opening so geckos don't scrape their noses during the shedding process. For large geckos over 90 grams we also recommend grinding out the cave opening a bit to allow easier access. We use these caves in the back of all our tubs as well as in terrariums. They provide a good stable hide and keep the temperature of the floor of the warm hide very constant. They are a bit heavy, so please use caution when lifting and replacing these caves so you don't drop them and possibly injure your gecko.

For dishes, the best on the market for leopard geckos are clear glass pyrex lab grade petri dishes, size 3160-60. They are very cleanable, break resistant, and geckos can see the mealworms easily which stimulates their feeding response. Petri dishes come with a top and bottom, with the top being shallower in depth. Use the tops for your supplement mixture and the bottoms for mealworms and water.

For hatchlings and small juveniles use the tops for easier access until the gecko is about 10-12 grams in size.

There are many accessories for those who wish to dress up their terrarium and use some enrichment for the gecko. Do not use wood or rocks from the outdoors unless you thoroughly wash and sterilize them. They could harbor bacteria and other organisms that are pathogenic to your gecko.

Pet stores offer a wide array of wood branches, artificial plants, and various other items that can create a very nice setting and give your gecko some things to explore and climb around on.

Firefox. Accessories used in leopard gecko habitats should consist of artificial plants only, and washed, sterilized items to prevent possible infection from pathogens foreign to them.

CHAPTER 8

Water and Supplementation

This chapter is one of the most important areas that needs to be emphasized. Lack of clean water and proper supplements are one of the most common causes of illness in leopard geckos. Leos do not drink a great deal of water, but the water they do drink needs to be clean and fresh at all times. Water dishes should be scrubbed out or changed at least every other day and refilled. Dirty water is teeming with bacteria and can cause significant health issues.

I also recommend the use of bottled spring water rather than tap water to avoid the consumption of chlorine and other compounds found in the tap water of many areas. I recall reading a study that found over 2000 compounds in solution in a sample of drinking water, including many pesticides, heavy metals, solvents, and even prescription drugs. Bottled water is inexpensive and worth the extra effort...it also contains beneficial minerals like calcium and magnesium.

In our production area, dirty petri dishes are soaked for at least 15 minutes, and usually overnight, in a germicidal solution, they are then rinsed and soaked again in hot soapy water and hand scrubbed, then rinsed very thoroughly to be sure all soap residues have been removed. While this is labor intensive, it's well worth the effort and will go a long way to keep your geckos healthy. Pyrex petri dishes are also very durable and can even be washed in high temperature automatic dish washers, but hand scrubbing is the best method to get the dishes as clean as possible.

It is best not to use RO or distilled water because they lack the nutrients of bottled spring water. Spring water is generally less than one dollar a gallon, and for the average gecko keeper a gallon will last a long time, and is well worth it.

As for supplements, it is imperative to properly administer vitamins and minerals as part of the animal's daily diet, particularly so for young geckos. We use a mixture of calcium with D3 mixed 50-50 with a high quality reptile vitamin supplement blend.

Hatchlings and young juvenile geckos must have their mealworms dusted lightly so they are sure to consume enough of these vital supplements or they can easily get metabolic bone disease. This very serious affliction is an awful health tragedy for the animal, where their bones and joints get soft and they cannot stand or walk normally. It is very often irreversible, so prevention is the key.

We dust the mealworms with our mixture for all geckos up to 30 grams in size. After that, we provide a separate dish of the supplement mixture which the geckos will lap up as they intuitively know they need to.

Vitamin D3, which is actually a hormone called cholecalciferol, is naturally produced by the body via exposure to sunlight. In humans, there are vitamin D receptors in the skin (primarily in the arms and face) that produce this vital hormone. D3 is crucial for many processes in the body, particularly proper assimilation of calcium. While some gecko keepers provide D3 only occasionally, our work has shown it to be beneficial daily in their supplement mixture, with no toxicity or health issues. Many physicians are now recommending daily D3 for their patients because of its remarkable effects on overall health, not just on calcium assimilation, so it stands to reason that it will be equally beneficial to animals as well, particularly for leopard geckos that do not get sunlight exposure.

Egg laying females need a great deal of calcium to form firm, viable eggs, so dusting their food is a great idea, in addition to providing them their usual dish of supplements. It is also wise to feed laying females insects high in protein and calcium during the egg laying season. Many breeders use crickets, but our preference is dubia roaches, which are high in calcium and double the protein of crickets. More on this in the Feeding chapter.

Zorro Mandarin Designer. "Patches" is a very healthy, robust gecko that shows that with high quality husbandry and proper supplementation, geckos can be produced with outstanding colors, patterns, and body structure.

CHAPTER 9

Acclimation, Socialization, and Intelligence

When receiving new geckos, there should be a quarantine period enforced for 3-4 weeks if other established geckos are present. The gecko should be observed closely for health issues, diarrhea, etc. Ideally, a fresh stool sample should be analyzed at a vet clinic to be sure the gecko does not have one of the common parasites, like pinworms, which are unfortunately somewhat common in today's mass breeding wholesale reptile operations.

If there are established geckos present, always work on those first and the new gecko last, being sure to wash thoroughly after handling the new gecko and disinfecting implements. Also, remember that new geckos often do not eat for a period of days when introduced into a new environment.

The new gecko should not be disturbed for 2-3 weeks, except for cleaning and feeding. Some geckos socialize to humans more quickly than others, but it takes them time to acclimate to their new habitat, sounds, and smells, so it is best to leave them alone as much as possible during this period. It is particularly important for young children to understand this, because they are always anxious to hold and play with their new friend. It is fine to softly speak to the new gecko so it gets used to your voice. Geckos seem to like the human voice and it's soothing to them, but screaming children, barking dogs, and a noisy introduction can make the acclimation for this new gecko a very scary and difficult transition. The habitat should not be located in the proximity of an area where a dog could be barking, or where a cat may have access to the habitat. Remember that geckos are prey animals, so they are somewhat insecure to begin with, and loud noises or harsh music will be sure to make their acclimation very difficult.

Once your gecko has gone through its acclimation period and it is eating regularly, you may begin to carefully handle it for short periods of time, increasing in duration as the animal becomes calm and seems secure with handling. Use the hand over hand method to handle a new gecko so they don't fall off your hand as they move forward. If the gecko is on a surface like a couch and it starts to move away from you, place your hand in front of the gecko like a fence, and then pick it up to stop its advance. Never suddenly grab a gecko by the tail or it could detach.

Geckos become tame very quickly if you follow the proper acclimation procedures and gently work yourself into their lives. Once you gain their trust, they will quickly become a good friend that will bring you joy for many years.

I have worked with just about every type of small animal there is, and leopard geckos are my all-time favorite because of all their wonderful attributes. They really do remind me of little dogs in the way they bond to people, and many of them have levels of intelligence that will astound you if you take the time to work with them.

Many people who get a reptile for a pet think of it as a fun animal to have and observe, but unfortunately, few people realize how really social reptiles can be. Leopard geckos are one of the smartest and most social of all the reptiles. You must work with them and have patience, much like you would with training a puppy. Geckos do not learn on their own, so we are their teachers. I have spent years working on the socialization aspects of geckos and have been amazed at just how smart they really are.

Leopard geckos have a very intuitive intelligence as well. They recognize their owners and those they like and are familiar with, and conversely react rather uneasily if they are in the presence of people who they sense fear from. In our store, it has been a great learning experience seeing how geckos reacted to different kinds of people. If customers were good, caring types of people, the geckos would react very favorably and let these people handle them easily. If someone came into the store who was of questionable character or acted erratically, loudly, or exhibited strange behavior of some sort, the geckos didn't want them to handle them or even get near them. Their intuition amazes me.

Some geckos are sometimes not genetically predisposed to be social, such as Enigmas, Eclipses/Raptors, Blazing Blizzards, and some of the other morphs that would just as soon be left alone and often don't really bond readily to people, though there are exceptions. As for regular intelligence, some geckos are smarter than others, as with all animal species. I have found the Giants, Snows, Tangerines, Designers, and Bandits, among others, to generally be easier to socialize and have somewhat higher levels of intelligence than some other morphs.

I have worked with many geckos to see just how much they can learn, the best way to teach them, and how to get them to recognize boundaries, and they never cease to amaze me. I have trained geckos to sit on the couch, watch TV, enjoy a warm cozy fire by the fireplace, and in general just observe the family activities around them. They will sit on the couch and never leave the boundaries of that couch, for hours! This is actually pretty easy to teach them if you are patient with them. Of course, it has to be the right type of gecko, with a calm personality and a good intelligence level to start with.

Gecko watching television. This is an amazing picture of one of my Super Giant couch buddies. When we were watching the Super Bowl, he crawled across the couch, got up onto the arm, and was riveted like this to the TV for 4 straight hours without moving! Incredible but true story.

Geckos, once mature, will almost never defecate outside their enclosure, so they are very clean animals that can sit on the couch or even bed, and respect that area as a duty-free zone! It is extremely rare for a gecko to have an accident once they are socialized, again, much like a dog.

So if you have a gecko that you feel has the right attributes for this type of socialization, then you can proceed with training them to respect boundaries. While sitting on the couch, allow the gecko to walk around on the chair or couch and explore, the whole time supervising them closely so they don't wander outside your chosen boundaries for them. If they move to the edge of those boundaries, firmly but gently push them back with your open hand onto the acceptable area and say "Nnnooo", much like how you would train a puppy. Continue to use that technique each time it strays to an area like the edge of the couch where you don't want it to go. If they misbehave continually, pick them up and immediate put them back into their habitat. They are smart animals, and in time they not only learn the boundary technique, but they also learn that if they misbehave you will put them away. Also, if they stray to the edge of the boundary and start to leave the designated area, but turn around when you call to them and go back onto the acceptable area, respond quickly by saying "good boy, or girl" just as you would a puppy. They learn to understand these phrases as positive reinforcement and learn the boundaries quickly if you use this technique properly.

Geckos love to be out doing people things like sitting on the couch watching TV, so they will quickly learn that if they behave they get to stay out more. I have trained even difficult macho males that I thought might be hopeless, into being perfect little angels on the couch. This process take patience and time, but is well worth the effort. The result will be a great couch buddy for years to come.

Many leopard geckos love to be handled and socialize very well to humans. Handling
them regularly and having fun with them enriches their lives and helps them to develop
their personalities. You'll be amazed at just how intelligent and playful
they are if you spend the time with them.

When I tell people how trainable they really are, I get the looks...but then
I'll see them a few months later and they tell me how incredible it is that their
gecko sits on the couch and watches TV with them! It's always funny, and grat-
ifying, to see that expression of excitement.

Rather than just having a beautiful little lizard in a nice terrarium, they suddenly have a real friend that they can hang out with, like a little lap dog. This
makes the whole experience even better, not only for the people, but for the
geckos who get to watch TV or sit by a nice warm fire and share in the banter
of the humans making funny talking sounds.

Geckos that have a good intelligence level can become very smart, even rec-
ognizing certain words and phrases. The soothing phrases like "good boy",

"good girl", "it's OK", "come here" and other phrases you might use with your dog can also be learned by some geckos. I have trained geckos to come to me when I call their names. It's a funny thing how many of them come when called. For instance, if I'm on the couch and they are at the other end of the couch and I call their name and tell them to come to me, they sometimes come right away, but often they will wait about 10 seconds, and then come to me. It's like they don't want to seem too anxious, and they want it to look like it was their idea to come and not mine....or maybe they just need to think about it for a while and then they decide to respond.

I recall a few very special incidents I will relay here as examples of their intelligence and intuition. Both of these events happened while my wife was lying in bed, and had a gecko with her on the bedspread while watching TV. One of our big Super Giant males, Ronnie, was sitting close to her but facing away from her so he could watch TV. I walked in and said how good he was being hanging out with her and watching TV so calmly and attentively. Then she said, "Yeah, but I only get to look at his backside!" Within one second of her saying that, Ronnie did a 180 and faced her up close and personal, as if to say "Sorry, is this better?" It was incredible to see and we were both flabbergasted. It was a special gecko moment we'll never forget, and it showed just how smart geckos really are. Maybe it was a coincidence, but since we've seen geckos do many things like this, I am led to believe that there's much more to these animals than just a pretty lizard in a terrarium.

Another incident was also stunning for us to witness. Carol was again in bed, this time with our star Bandit gecko, Zorro, who was sitting on the bedspread watching TV. We were talking about making a major life decision to move out of state. Carol then said, the move would be tough for us, but the most difficult thing to think about is, what are we going to do with all these geckos?!

Immediately after she said that, Zorro walked over to her very deliberately, and put his front paw on her hand, as if to comfort her and tell her not to worry and that it would be OK to take them. He stood there motionless like a statue for about five minutes with his one paw on her hand. It was a moving thing to experience, and again, maybe it was coincidence, but it seemed so purposeful that we couldn't help but think that on some level, he understood what she said and he wanted to reassure her that it would be OK.

Perhaps the most incredible example of gecko intelligence occurred when Ronnie was on the bedspread with Carol one night when she had just gotten a new IPad and was using it to do some internet surfing. Ronnie watched her intently, when suddenly he walked over to her, climbed onto the IPad screen, and started swiping at the screen repeatedly with his right paw, seemingly trying to make the screen change! He did this rapid swiping motion on the screen with his paw for several seconds, as if to amuse himself, and us. It was an incredible event that we were both lucky enough to witness. He saw her doing this so he thought he'd give it a try. And no, we did not go out and buy him his own IPad!

I know this all likely sounds all too contrived, but these types of things happen a lot with us as we pursue our enrichment and socialization studies on these wonderful little animals. Suffice it to say that if you are willing to spend the time with them the sky's the limit. Again, it's important to note that geckos have varying degrees of intelligence. Some of this is morph/genetic dependent, and some is just the gecko's own personality. ...some are just more playful and attentive than others. One thing we have noticed is that these types of personality traits and intelligence levels are very often passed down to the offspring. Smart geckos produce smart offspring. I've always found it incredible how much geckos will act and even have feeding habits like their parents. The day will come when breeders will take these factors into account in their breedings, just as much as color, size, or any other genetic trait.

Now, not all geckos have the propensity to be a super intelligent animal with outstanding socialized behavior patterns, just as not all dogs will be show dogs or all horses will be blue ribbon champions. The key is to select geckos based on breeding and parental temperament, and then to spend the time and effort with them, and have great patience. If you have the right gecko, the payoff is worth it.

If your goal is to have a beautiful, high quality gecko that you can have as a showpiece animal and perhaps breed, then the above parameters may not necessarily be of importance to you. But if you do choose to pursue a highly socialized gecko with superior intellect, then you must select based on the described criteria and hope for the best. Your commitment to the training is the most necessary ingredient.

Hot Moose Super Giant. Giants are among the most docile and intelligent morphs.

Another thing we have found beneficial for enrichment and socialization is the use of low level soft music in the gecko room. I first got this idea of music enrichment back in my career in pharmaceutical research. Laboratory rabbits are known to be very sensitive to stressors in a research setting and often have diarrhea issues and weight loss due to the stress of the lab experience. I decided to try low level easy listening radio stations in the rabbit rooms to see if it had any effect on perhaps soothing and calming them. To our amazement, the rabbits all became very calm and easy to handle, and the diarrhea stopped completely.

It was amazing that a simple thing like this would have such a dramatic physiological effect on the rabbits. They all became very friendly and would come to the front of their cages wanting to be picked up and handled. Music became part of our research program from that point on.

To follow through with that theory, I also decided to use it in my gecko production rooms, with equally amazing results. Geckos spend a lot of time lying in their enclosures, and individually housed, so the music gives them something to hear and broadens their experience.

I believe this helps greatly with socialization, because then they also hear people on the radio talking and they get used to the music, and the people's voices. Everyone has always commented on how calm our geckos are and I think the use of low level radio is a big factor. I encourage anyone who has geckos to try this enrichment aspect, being sure that you select an easy listening, soft rock, or classical station in your area without a lot of talking or commercials. All areas have stations like this so find the right one and give it a try. I especially encourage breeders to use radio enrichment in their production area. And remember no hard rock...take it easy... Remember, John Denver or Eagles good, Led Zeppelin or rap, not so much! A television in an animal room is an excellent idea to give them something to watch while in their enclosures. Many large animal research facilities use television as a source of enrichment for animals to alleviate stress, with excellent results. I witnessed a primate room at a facility where they used television for enrichment and it was remarkable to see how much the animals enjoyed watching TV. (Sesame Street tapes were their favorite!)

Geckos grow to love their human family, and will crave human attention. When they want to be handled, they'll make it very evident usually by coming out of their caves when you are around, or standing up in the front corners of their habitat. They are showing you that they'd like to get some attention, so take the time to pick them up at that time and say hello. Make it a positive experience each time they crave attention, and they will quickly learn that you are their buddy and they will want to see you more and more. I always encourage people to talk to their geckos. Speak softly and let them know you care about them. They understand more than you might realize.

Super Giant. "T Rex" shows how geckos appreciate a nice habitat. The Giants have a very mellow temperament, making them an ideal pet gecko for those looking for a larger animal.

While it is great to be a breeder and it's exciting to spread the joy of your work to others who will acquire a lifelong friend that you produced, it is also nice to just have one or two geckos. While breeding is exciting, it limits you as to how much attention you can give the geckos due to the workload and hours required to run a breeding operation or care for a large collection. When you just have one or a few geckos, you can really spend a lot of time with them and that's when you really get amazing results with your socialization efforts.

In recent years, several studies have been done on reptile intelligence, showing that indeed, reptiles are very intelligent. This trend in studies will continue, and hopefully someday, an in-depth study will be done on leopard geckos which will point out just how smart these lizards really are. In the past, many studies have been done on animals that equates brain size to intelligence, however that should be debunked based on the fact that horses are extremely intelligent and their brain is only the size of a walnut! Intuitive intelligence as shown in leopard geckos, is something that can be difficult to measure, but my limited study work in our own experience shows that they think, reason, and solve problems at an amazing level.

Some geckos can be trained to ride on your shoulder. They seem to enjoy that lofty location, but you must proceed with caution as a fall from that level could result in a serious injury. But once you and the gecko master that technique and your gecko is secure on your shoulder, you can even go for walks with them outside as long as the weather is appropriate and you are very careful.

The bottom line is, don't limit yourself in your gecko experience. There's a great big world out there to explore with your new friend, and you'll both have a very happy and rewarding experience if you take the time to let them show you just how special they really are.

Tangerines. Geckos are very peaceful, social, and intelligent animals that respond to high quality care and attention. Take the time to train and socialize your gecko, and you will both have a fun and rewarding life together.

CHAPTER 10

Feeding

This could be the one of the most important chapters to peruse when learning about leopard gecko care. I have spent a great deal of time and effort examining and learning about the feeding behavior of leopard geckos, and it can be more complex than just putting a few mealworms in a dish for them. It is always wise when purchasing a new gecko to ask the breeder what it prefers to eat and what its feeding habits are. An ethical breeder will be honest and give you accurate information, which will be an immense help when selecting a gecko and transitioning it into your care.

Feeding geckos can be one of the most problematic issues for people when they get a new gecko, so it is best to establish all of this properly right from the start. If possible, it is ideal to obtain geckos that have been raised on mealworms, as those are the easiest to transition to other feeder insects if you choose to. Geckos raised on crickets often will only eat crickets and generally will not be very willing to eat anything else.

First off, there are basically three types of geckos when considering feeding behavior...normal eaters, ravenous eaters, and picky eaters. Normal eaters are geckos that will generally accept any type of feeder insect from time to time, but not necessarily with consistency. Some normal eaters will accept mealworms as their regular staple diet, and will also occasionally eat other types of feeder insects. They will generally be good eaters all the time, taking periodic breaks from eating, which is totally normal. Ravenous eaters are a gecko keeper's dream, because they will eat anything, anytime, anywhere. They will accept any type of feeder insect, and are always ready and willing to devour anything you offer them. The downside of this type is that they can get obese very quickly, so the keeper has to be very diligent in monitoring and controlling their food intake.

Once a gecko gets obese and gets a very heavy tail, it is extremely difficult to ever get them back to a normal weight again, short of starving them, which of course is never advisable. Feeding in a very controlled way is crucial to geckos that are ravenous eaters.

Picky eaters are difficult to cope with for many hobbyists. Geckos like this are always a challenge, and can be very frustrating to deal with for even very experienced keepers. All geckos have their own individualized food preferences, so experiment with various insects until you hit on the right one. Picky eaters should also be evaluated for possible parasite issues, and their habitat needs to be reviewed to ensure their conditions are optimal, particularly temperatures within their enclosure and warm hide surface.

Mature geckos in particular can have very specific insect favorites, so it is advisable to spend some time to ascertain what that preference is. Not all geckos will eat everything. Many geckos also take food breaks during winter months when they go into a sort of winter dormancy, a slowdown period when they sense cooler temperatures and shorter days, and their metabolism slows as it would in the wild. Normal eaters follow this pattern of periodic breaks in eating. This does not present any problems as long as the body weight doesn't drop significantly and the tail maintains a decent amount of fat reserve. If the tail starts looking thin and spiny, it may be time to stimulate their appetite to get them back into a normal feeding pattern again.

When a gecko has been off food for a period of time, its production of digestive enzymes and stomach acid is greatly reduced, which curbs their appetite. What you need to do to stimulate their appetite is to get them to eat something that they may be interested in. Once they eat, their stomach starts to function normally and the hunger urge returns, putting them back into a normal feeding pattern. There are several methods to accomplish this. The use of fresh waxworms can often get a gecko enticed to eating again. While many oppose the use of waxworms saying they are too high in fat, like candy, I have found them to be an extremely beneficial feeder insect in geckos that have gone a long period without eating and have lost appreciable weight. Geckos often find waxworms irresistible, and once they eat a few, you can often get them back to eating normally again with their previous staple of mealworms or superworms. Waxworms can also be problematic however, as they can be addictive in a sense and the geckos sometimes won't eat anything else after being on waxworms.

The key is to just feed waxworms over a period of a few days, and then quickly try to transition them back onto their normal feeder insect.

Other things can also be tried to entice a gecko to eat again. Freshly shed, white superworms or white dubia roaches can be very tempting to geckos that have been off food.

I prefer to tong feed superworms and dubias at the warm cave opening. Tong feeding is very beneficial, as superworms and dubias can be fast and quickly crawl under the substrate, creating more work for you and an impossible insect for the gecko to find. Tong feeding is very effective, but be sure to use blunt tipped forceps. Geckos can very aggressively grab insects from the forceps which can injure the soft tissues of the mouth and cause injury and possible infection, so never use sharp forceps when feeding reptiles of any kind.

Another very effective method of stimulating appetite is with the use of crickets, preferably de-legged. I do not normally recommend feeding crickets to leopard geckos for many reasons. Crickets can generally be a rather dirty insect, and can harbor a high bacterial load and possibly even pathogenic organisms. Crickets smell really bad after a day or two in an enclosure, not pleasant to have around the average household! They are much more expensive than mealworms and superworms, and they can get loose in the house, and chirp and drive you crazy. In some areas where scorpions are problematic, having a colony of crickets in your house is a sure invitation for scorpions, which regard crickets as their favorite food.

Now, crickets can also be an excellent way to get geckos eating again who've been off food for a prolonged time. The best way to accomplish this, is to buy a small quantity of crickets, provide them with gutload and fresh carrot, and carefully remove their rear jumping legs with forceps. Then place the de-legged crickets into a small dish near the warm hide opening, or try tong feeding them. Geckos will often eat them quickly, and once they do, you have stimulated their appetite and metabolism and you can then transition them to other feeders.

If all these methods fail, your habitat parameters are correct, and you've determined that parasites are not an issue, then you need to take more drastic action to save the gecko from succumbing to its anorexia. This method involves the use of a 1cc syringe, and careful handling techniques. Mix chicken baby food (with broth type, not gravy type) from a jar with a small amount of spring water and some of the geckos normal supplement mixture and stir thoroughly to make a slurry of the mixture. Draw 1cc of this slurry into the syringe. Hold the gecko carefully but very firmly in your fist so just its head is protruding from your hand, and hold it until it settles down in your hand. Then with your other hand, slide the tip of the syringe back and forth along the jaw line until the gecko opens its mouth a bit. Slide the tip of the syringe carefully into the gecko's mouth and slowly inject the contents into the mouth. Once you perfect this technique, it is very easy to administer.

The geckos often like the chicken and will take it more willingly the next time. Repeat this procedure daily for 3-5 days. Then try to introduce insects in the dish as normal and see if the gecko will begin to eat on its own again. If after a few days it still has not eaten insects, repeat the syringe method again for a few days, and repeat the feeding attempts. Another excellent syringe food choice is A/D canned diet for cats and dogs. It is a complete diet and can be used instead of chicken. Most vet offices will have A/D diet on hand, and I highly recommend it for this purpose because of its very complete nutritional content.

Hand feeding or assist feeding is another very important technique to master as you grow in your gecko hobby pursuits, particularly if you plan to do breedings and produce hatchlings. If syringe feeding is something you prefer not to do or is difficult for you to master, another great technique to jumpstart a gecko's appetite is assist feeding. In this method, you hold the gecko in your hand as you would in syringe feeding, take an appropriately sized waxworm or mealworm in a forceps, and slowly rub the insect along the mouth of the gecko until it opens the mouth. Carefully insert the insect into the mouth, and if necessary hold the gecko's mouth closed with your fingertips until the gecko has swallowed. Repeat this method, trying to get the gecko to eat 2-3 insects in succession, then put it back into its enclosure. Repeat this procedure daily for 3-4 days, until the gecko begins to eat on its own from its dish.

White and Yellow. This beautiful hatchling will begin eating baby mealworms on its third or fourth day. Occasionally, hatchlings do not know how to eat on their own, so you need to take action if you observe this behavior. Once they are fed a few mealworms, they begin to eat on their own, but getting them started is the key.

Now that we have gone over some of the feeding idiosyncrasies of geckos, it's time to discuss the various feeder insect choices. Always feed your insects fresh, organic produce. Healthy feeder insects produce healthy geckos. Pesticide residue, even in miniscule amounts, is not healthy for the insects or your gecko. I always recommend using organic oat bran for bedding in mealworms and superworms. Many recommend wheat bran, but many animals have allergies to wheat so it is not advisable to take chances with your gecko by using it either. Oat bran is readily available at most health food stores. Waxworms are housed with egg crate and wood chips or shavings and do not need to be gutloaded.

- *Mealworms.* The most widely used insect feeder for leopard geckos is the mealworm. Mealworms are inexpensive, readily available, clean with no odor, and when gutloaded properly are a complete diet for geckos. It is best to purchase your mealworms (or any feeder insects) from well established, reliable sources. Online vendors will ship them right to your doorstep. Be sure to order mealworms when the weather is moderate, not too cold or hot.

I put all of our geckos on mealworms as hatchlings through adulthood. This not only is nutritionally effective and an easy insect to feed to large numbers of geckos, but it allows our customers to have a much simpler experience feeding a gecko that has been raised on mealworms. As a gecko matures, monitor their food intake closely, and watch their weight using the tail girth as a gauge as mealworms do have a fairly significant fat content. Some geckos (ravenous eaters) will eat all you'll give them, so don't overdo it with kindness. They may look up at you like they are starving, begging for food, but overfeeding geckos is never a good idea.

Fully mature, adult geckos may only need to eat a few times a week. Young geckos need to eat daily, and make sure their insects are dusted lightly with the supplement mixture to promote good health and strong bone and joint structure, and prevent metabolic bone disease. There is nothing sadder to see than a lizard with MBD, so please don't let this happen to your gecko.

Baby geckos should be fed small or baby mealworms for the first two weeks. After they have been eating consistently and are starting to grow, you can gradually feed them larger mealworms of appropriate size. Occasionally, baby geckos do not know how to eat on their own. When that happens you must take immediate action by using the previously discussed assist feeding method using baby mealworms with forceps.

Handle babies with great care and caution as they are very fragile. After a few days of assist feeding, young geckos will start to eat mealworms on their own.

Note that hatchlings do not eat for their first 3-4 days until after their first shed. (Always provide moisture for hatchling geckos up to 14 days of age to facilitate their first few sheds.)

Please follow these instructions to keep your mealworms healthy:

Mealworms must be refrigerated so they do not turn into pupae and beetles. When you refrigerate your mealworms, be sure you do not place the container in the super cold zone of the refrigerator (the ideal storage temperature for mealworms and waxworms is 50^0F). Also, be sure you have air holes in the container so the mealworms can breathe even though they are dormant in the fridge. A small tupperware container with holes in the top works very well. Use organic oat bran as the bedding for your mealworms.

Every two weeks, take the container out of the fridge, sprinkle a thin layer of insect food on the surface, and place some fresh organic carrots sliced lengthwise in with the mealworms. Leave the container out at room temperature for 24 hours so the mealworms can eat. After 24 hours, remove the carrots and place the container back into the fridge. This will keep your mealworms fed and healthy for months.

Every 3-4 days, take out as many mealworms as you'll need to feed your gecko for that period of time, place them in a small bowl, put in some insect food and fresh organic carrot slices daily, and leave that dish at room temp....these gutloaded mealworms are what you will feed to your gecko. For young geckos, be sure to put a pinch of your mineral/vitamin mixture in their mealworm dish so your growing gecko gets enough of those important supplements.

Also discard any black or dried out mealworms. If any mealworms turn into white pupae, discard those as well since the gecko will not eat them.

- *Dubia roaches*. Dubia roaches are a wonderful feeder insect, are easy to handle, they don't bite or pinch, have minimal odor, do not climb up plastic or fly, and are chock full of nutrients and 36% protein (double the protein of crickets). Not all geckos will eat dubias, but the ones that do get very healthy and robust. Egg laying females willing to eat dubias produce excellent quality eggs and offspring.

Dubias (of appropriate size) should always be tong fed to your gecko individually to avoid escapees and to make feeding your gecko a much simpler process. Remember to use blunt tipped or curve tipped forceps whenever tong feeding to avoid mouth injuries.

Dubia roaches should be fed a good quality grain gutload, dry cat or dog food of good quality, and supplemented with fresh organic produce like kale, carrots, and orange sections. Dubias love oranges and that not only is very healthy for them and your geckos due to the high vitamin C content, but it also seems to boost dubia reproduction rates, likely because of the sugar content. While many use water crystals in the dubia enclosures, I've found crystals to be very messy, which promotes bacterial and mold growth...not good. Using fresh, lengthwise cut carrots, replaced daily, will give them all the water and humidity they need. We've raised dubia for years in this way with excellent results and a high reproduction rate.

Dubias can be housed in plastic tubs with egg crate material at room temperature, and need a warm area of 90^0F to thrive and reproduce, so you can house them in a gecko rack or a tub with an under tank heat pad regulated at 90^0F. Clean the frass out regularly and wipe out the tub periodically with paper towels and water (no cleaning compounds) to provide a good environment for your dubia colony, which will promote good growth and reproduction rates. Freshly shed white roaches are soft and a delicacy for geckos, so feed the white roaches to your picky eaters who will likely relish them. Dubia roaches are an outstanding feeder insect and we encourage hobbyists to give them a try.

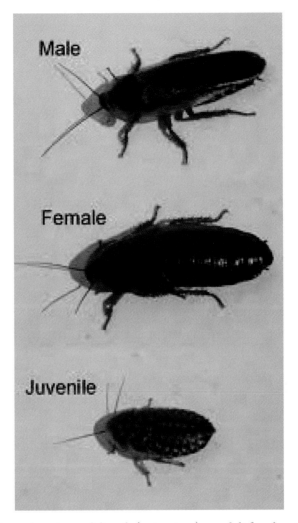

Dubia roaches. Shown here is an adult male (note wings), an adult female, and a juvenile.
The ideal size to feed leopard geckos is 1/2 to 1 inch depending on the size of the gecko.
Dubias are very high in protein and calcium, prolific breeders,
easy to care for, and an excellent quality feeder insect.

- *Superworms.* Superworms are an excellent feeder insect, high in calories, and are easy to keep. Superworms can be easily stored at room temperature and will not pupate as long as they are group housed. Store them in oat bran bedding with some egg crate on top and provide lengthwise sliced carrots on top of the bedding daily. They also will eat orange quarters, potatoes, kale, and other produce. Superworms are fairly large, and one is equal to many mealworms, so one superworm a day is likely all you should feed the average gecko, cutting back to one every 2-3 days when the gecko is mature or they can get obese quickly on supers. As with all feeder insects, some geckos eat them and some will not. It is important to find what a gecko's preference is and feed them what they want, trying to vary it now and then if they are willing.

Super worms are a relatively inexpensive insect to obtain, and you can usually buy large quantities quite reasonably on the internet. Avoid shipping in cold or hot weather as they are sensitive to temperature extremes. The best way to feed superworms is by tong feeding, or dropping a superworm in front of the gecko or at the entrance to its warm hide. If the gecko does not eat the superworm immediately, remove it from the enclosure or it can be a nuisance to the gecko and turn it off of food. Geckos that eat superworms can get very obese quickly so watch that they are not overfed.

Be sure a superworm does not get loose in your home. As individuals, they pupate, turn into a beetle, and then produce a very offensive odor like a burned electrical like smell. The smell can linger for long periods of time.

- *Waxworms.* These little white moth larvae are a very misunderstood insect. Purist gecko keepers rant about the use of waxworms because of their fat content and addictive aspects. Geckos love them, so they can get hooked on them quickly to the point that it is difficult to get them to eat anything else. However, there are times when waxworms can save the day for geckos who are in an anorexic phase for some reason or other and are dropping weight. If a gecko refuses to eat its normal insect diet and is dropping weight and losing its tail fat quickly, using fresh, juicy waxworms can turn a potential tragedy into a feeding frenzy. Use waxworms with caution, and try to switch them back onto other feeders as soon as possible. Sometimes, if the gecko is devouring the waxworms as quickly as you can drop them in front of them, it's a great time to drop in a mealworm too. After a few sessions of that, you can often get them back onto mealworms.

Obtaining fresh waxworms can be a challenge. There are a few excellent online sources, and always again be sure to avoid weather extremes when ordering a shipment. Waxworms do not need to be gutloaded since they are a larva that feeds off of its own fat stores. They ideally should be stored at 50^0F in small wood chips or shavings and a piece of egg crate on top. If stored in this way, waxworms can last for several weeks.

While I do not recommend them as steady diet, they can be a nice occasional treat and definitely have their place when your gecko refuses to eat anything else.

- *Other feeder insects.* There are many other feeders on the market, but generally, they are not well liked by the majority of geckos. Butterworms, hornworms, and others can be worth a try, but our studies have shown that they are not great for leos. Butterworms seem to produce indigestion for geckos who often regurgitate them. Silkworms are an excellent insect and very high in calcium, but they get mixed results and are very hard to obtain and keep alive for more than a few days. Do not feed live caught insects to your gecko as they could harbor pathogens or have pesticide residue.

NUTRITIONAL ANALYSIS					
	Crickets	Meal Worms	Wax Worms	Super Worms	Dubia Roach
Moisture, %	69.07	62.44	61.73	59.37	61.8
Fat, %	6.01	12.72	22.19	17.89	6.75
Protein, %	21.32	20.27	15.50	17.41	35.6
Fiber, %	3.2	1.73	7.69	6.80	3.25
Ash	2.17	1.57	1.02	1.20	2.01
Ca, ppm	345	133	283	124	~500
P, ppm	4238	3345	2161	2320	
CA/P ratio %	0.081	0.040	0.131	0.053	

Nutritional chart courtesy Grubco Inc. (with added Dubia values)

Breeding, Eggs, and Hatchling Care

Various methods are used by reptile breeders, and each has its merits. The same holds true for the care of eggs and their incubation. Whatever method works for them is fine of course, and many breeders have tremendous success and productivity using their own individualized methods. I will describe my preferred methodologies in this chapter that I have had good success with so it can be used as an adjunct to your own breeding program if you choose to.

I am extremely particular on how I breed my geckos and how I raise the eggs to hatchlings, and beyond. Colony breedings are the norm for many breeders, which often times means placing a male in with a group of females, providing a large lay box for the females, and harvesting the eggs as they are produced. There are downsides to this method. Males can get very aggressive when placed with females, and I have seen large production facilities using this method and having females with lost tails, lacerations, and even eyes missing in their colony breedings.

Another downside to this method is in not necessarily knowing the exact genetics of the eggs you are harvesting from a mass lay box. If all females have the exact same genetic background, then it is possible to generalize the genetics of the eggs produced in a given colony. The other factor is, if you produce a few very spectacular offspring from a colony, or some variation that is highly desirable, you would have no idea who the exact parents were that produced that outcome so you could try to track that and reproduce the result. I have seen breeders harvesting eggs and placing them all in a big pile at one time, then putting them into cups for incubation. Of course, they have no real idea what they are going to hatch from which egg, and that leads to guesswork based on what the hatchling looks like.

Production practices like this can muddy up the genetic pool worldwide, and that is something that I wish breeders would take into consideration when using these methods. This has been a concern of mine, and other specialty breeders for years, and yet these practices continue.

While genetic background mistakes can happen, I'm not sure why some don't take greater precautions to try to minimize these variables that have become more and more common as more people try their hands at breeding reptiles.

My method, while perhaps not as productive in numbers as colony breedings, is to do individual breedings so that I know the exact parents of each egg produced. While some breeders feel that females can be bred at 45 grams, I prefer them to be at least 60 grams so they are more developed and mature to handle the egg production and laying process. Leo eggs are quite large and egg binding of young females can be extremely dangerous to the health of the female.

For the mating process, I place a male and female in a large tub covered with paper liners on the floor securely taped down so the geckos have great traction during the mating process. I observe the mating carefully. If the female is not ovulating or receptive, a fight can ensue immediately, and I quickly intervene and end the battle, and remove the female (watch out for bites) and try again a few days later. Sometimes a male and female will fight and one locks onto another like a pit bull and will not let go. It is good to have a tub close by with a couple inches of water in it, so if this happens you can scoop up the embattled pair and place them in the water so they release their bite and minimize any potential damage.

If the female is ovulating and receptive, the male will gently bite the female up and down her body during the process, they will mate, and the male will then turn around and clean himself. Once completed, the male is removed and placed back in his tub. The female is then placed back in her tub, with a label indicating the male and his genetics, and the date of the mating. If you have placed a male and female together, and think that they have bred but are unsure, you can separate them and then try to put them back together a few days later. If the female strongly refuses the male's advances, she is likely already pregnant.

All of my geckos are individually housed, and while this takes up a lot of valuable space, I know exactly what the matings were and who the parents are of each and every egg. This breeding specificity is very valuable and takes the guesswork out of the entire breeding process.

This single breeding method is a huge benefit to those obtaining geckos from such breedings because the exact genetics of the offspring are known if they choose to breed these geckos at some point themselves.

Keeping good records of all breedings is essential for the serious breeder. I track the date and male of each breeding by placing a label on each female's tub. On the same label, I track each lay date and how many good eggs were produced on that date.

Mandarin Tangerines. These hatchlings, line bred offspring and clutchmates of Mandarin and his mother, are genetically very similar but very different in coloration. As they mature, both will be very orange, with the darker brother being a deeper, more intense orange. These hatchlings point out the huge benefits of single breedings and scrupulous egg tracking to be able to very accurately determine lineage and be able to try to duplicate results in future breedings.

Lay boxes can be simple tupperware type containers with a horseshoe shaped hole in the side at the top, and our studies have found moist coconut fiber works best. Many use moss for their lay boxes, but that produces significant odor in a production area so I prefer the coconut fiber and have had excellent success with it. It should be kept slightly moist but not wet.

Be careful not to allow the fiber to completely dry out as that would allow the eggs to stick to the plastic lay box, risking perforating the eggs when you try to un-stick them.

Eggs laid outside the lay box are generally not viable eggs and can be discarded. Females know if the eggs they are producing are not good and will instinctively lay the eggs outside the lay box, on the paper liner, or even in their water dish.

When removing eggs from the laybox, they must be handled very carefully and not jostled or dropped. I then place the eggs in an egg container that has segregated partitions so each and every egg has its own compartment. I chart out every egg container so I know which egg went into each sector, the date it was laid, and the exact parents of that egg. This takes all the guesswork out of the process, and when the baby hatches I know the exact genetics of that baby. All information is carefully recorded, and these records are kept for years so we can refer back to them as needed.

The eggs can be carefully marked with a small line using a Sharpie marker on the top center so the eggs position is always oriented properly. Once eggs are placed in their container, they should not be moved or jarred as drowning of the embryo can occur. Females will generally lay 2 eggs at a time, and mature females can lay from 6-16 eggs in a season. Each clutch of two eggs are laid approximately 14-21 days apart. First year females may only lay infertile eggs for their first clutch or two. Females are most productive from their second to sixth year of age.

Viable eggs are firm to the touch and are well formed. If eggs are very soft, dented, or collapsed when laid, they are not viable and should be discarded. As eggs are incubated, if they begin to turn brown or form mold, they are not good eggs and should be removed from the container immediately so they don't contaminate other eggs.

Egg container labeling. Note that this container is labeled R1 and each egg has its own labeled sector. We make a chart for container R1, and record the exact parentage and lay date of each egg on that chart. This takes away guesswork and allows for accurate genetic tracking of every hatchling.

In the egg incubation containers themselves, I prefer using a hatching medium that is basically sterile and free from bacteria or mold spores. Perlite and vermiculite are fine, but have issues, so it is worth it to pay a little more for a high quality egg hatching media that will not put your eggs in jeopardy under very moist conditions. The media should be very moist but not dripping wet. You should place 8-10 holes with a pushpin in the lid for exchange of gases that will occur in the egg container environment. Check the container regularly, and if the media appears to be drying out, carefully add some distilled water to the container to saturate it, being careful not to get it too wet or get water on the eggs.

Using our incubation method, male eggs hatch in 35-40 days and females 55-60 days on average. Remember that it is important to keep adequate moisture in the incubator so condensation forms on the door as an indicator of adequate humidity. It is also essential to keep a very reliable digital thermometer in every incubator so that you always know the exact temperature within the cabinet at all times.

Never rely on the outside cabinet temperature readout of any incubator...this cannot be overemphasized. Temperature fluctuations and spikes can cause abnormalities in embryos such as various malformations and kinked tails, so careful temperature monitoring and stabilization is crucial.

I recommend having at least 4 incubators if you wish to be very particular about the egg process and produce high quality offspring. Eggs being incubated for male can be kept consistently at 90^0F for the duration, so this is easy to administer. Females on the other hand, require a different method of incubation if you want to do it right. This is where accurate records are essential as discussed earlier in this chapter.

Start out eggs incubating for female at 80^0 for 4 weeks to lock in the sex. Three weeks is not adequate and will produce several males, so lock the sex in at 4 weeks. After 4 weeks of incubation at 80^0, move the eggs to your next incubator set at 83^0-84^0 for a week. The move them up to 85-87^0 for the remainder of the time until they hatch. This will give you nice bright females, which is of particular importance when working with albino morphs.

Egg hatching. Here's a baby just coming into the world. They break through the shell with their egg tooth, catch their breath for a few minutes, and out they come... the miracle of life.

In 2013, I did a very critical study using this incubation temperature method, and I was astounded at the results...a 100% success rate on temperature sexing and no birth defects. This shows that with extremely careful incubation procedures and monitoring, this can be a very accurate and scientific process.

While some say that you need to spend several hundred dollars to get a good quality incubator, I have found the new, small cabinet incubators to actually be of high quality and produce excellent results, and at a very reasonable cost. Again, careful monitoring is essential, but if you take the time to do it right, you will have great success bringing beautiful, healthy geckos into the world.

Hatchlings. These two newborns are ready to be removed and placed into their tubs. All babies I raise are singly housed for better growth rates and socialization to humans. This takes up a lot of space but the results are worth it. The baby on the right is a son of the famous "Mandarin". The baby on the left is a Giant baby, so baby Mandarin was quite a big hatchling.

Many gecko hobbyists get so enthralled with the excitement of having these wonderful animals that they often want to start breeding projects of their own. It's important to take a step back and think about all the ramifications of breeding animals before one plunges into it. It is imperative that animal breeding is thoroughly researched before simply putting a male and female together to produce eggs. There are many things to consider. Humane breeding should be of the highest priority, and great care should be taken to ensure the safety of the animals to be bred. It is also of utmost importance to know that you will have an outlet or market for the geckos you will produce. So many who get into breeding just automatically think they can sell their geckos, without thinking of, to whom.

Many people will only buy geckos from well known, established breeders, which makes it difficult for budding gecko entrepreneurs to break into the business, even on a small scale. There are always large numbers of pet-quality geckos on the market, selling in the $10-30 range. Selling geckos at these prices is not cost effective for the average breeder, and the only guarantee you will have in breeding them is that you will lose money. I ask you to take the geckos into consideration and be sure you have a market before you produce them. There are reptile rescue operations around the world that are full of reptiles that need homes due in large part to overproduction, much as with cats and dogs at humane societies. Please take this into consideration.

Now, if you have done your research and are taking the plunge into breeding and know you have a market, it is time to learn how to care for the offspring you will produce.

Hatchling. This newborn Mandarin Enigma is as cute as they come, and she shows why so many want to do their own breeding projects. Note how delicate newborn's bone structure is, making extremely careful handling technique the #1 priority.

Baby geckos are quite hardy right from birth, but need to be handled carefully because they are still quite fragile in the first few weeks of life and can be injured if not handled with the utmost care. When taking babies out of the egg containers after hatching, rather than grabbing the baby and risking breaking a bone if it suddenly startles, it is best to use a small plastic spoon to lift the gecko gently into its new habitat.

Never handle baby geckos over a hard surface, and always take great care to set the cup into the new habitat so as not to risk dropping the baby and breaking a bone. Once the baby is in its new environment and you have recorded all pertinent information, it is best to leave the hatchling alone for the first 3-4 days, but observing them daily to be sure all's OK.

It is important to always provide a very moist environment for hatchlings for the first two weeks, as those initial sheds are crucial and moisture will be key to those sheds being successful with no remnants. Removing shed remnants from a hatchling is no easy chore and can result in injury, so be sure you provide daily moisture in their enclosure.

Baby leopard geckos will generally not eat for their first 3-4 days until after their first shed. After three days, you can place baby mealworms in a small shallow dish like a glass petri dish. Do not dust the first offering of mealworms to ensure that the hatchlings will eat. Once they are eating, then you must lightly dust the mealworms with a 50-50 mixture of calcium plus D3 and a high quality vitamin preparation.

Baby geckos' bones are forming, strengthening, and growing very fast, so they must have their feeder insects dusted. Once geckos are in the 25-30 gram range, you no longer need to dust their food but must provide a separate dish with this vitamin mineral mixture, which they will lap up as they intuitively know they need to.

Baby geckos should soon be eating on their own right after their first shed, but occasionally babies just don't know how to eat on their own, like baby birds. When you see that they are not eating and mealworms are not disappearing from their dish, it's time to take action as described in the previous chapter, and assist feed the babies with baby mealworms using that described method. After 2-3 days of assist feeding, they generally get the hang of it and will start to eat on their own from the dish.

It is very difficult for breeders to singly house hatchlings due to space constraints, but I've found that if you do, the geckos grow at an amazing rate and socialize to humans in a remarkable way. They socialize to humans very quickly and become wonderful adult geckos that are totally bonded to their human friends. I have experimented with various housing arrangements, and the babies that are housed singly mature in a much more social way and accept humans as their own family, the same as imprint animals. I highly recommend individual housing of geckos and even babies if you have space.

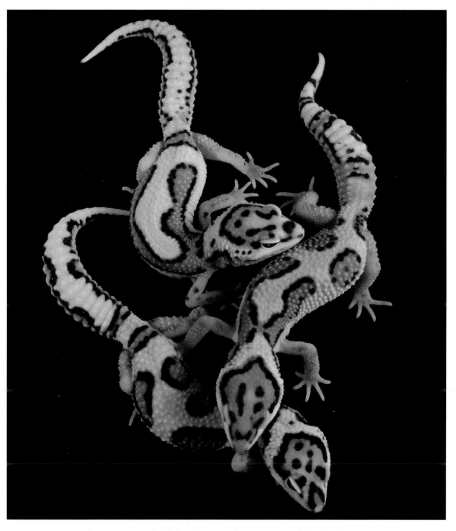

Producing geckos is a wonderful and rewarding aspect of the hobby, but be sure you have a market for the geckos you will produce before you move forward.

CHAPTER 12

Shipping and Receiving

Whether you plan to breed and sell geckos that will be shipped, or you are a hobbyist/collector that will be receiving animals via shipping couriers, there are some very important things to take into consideration. As stated ad infinitum, geckos, as with any animals that are shipped, rely on us for their safety and well-being. This is of paramount importance in shipping.

I have spent a great deal of time and effort to determine the best and safest methods because I wanted to ensure that we would never have problems with our shipping practices or put our animals in harm's way. I thus endeavored to do some critical studies on these methods.

First of all, it is imperative that appropriate shipping containers are used. Boxes must be durable and styrofoam lined, and should be obtained from reputable sources. The box you choose should be large enough to accommodate the number and size of deli cups you will be using in each shipment, allowing for the addition of heat packs or cold packs as needed depending on shipping conditions.

Backfill voids to be sure the cups are stable during shipment, and use crumpled paper as your backfill medium. The use of packing peanuts or plastic bubble wrap is generally not advised because potentially toxic fumes can be released when used in conjunction with heat packs.

Deli cups should be perforated to allow air exchange inside the cup, and the lid should be tight fitting and taped if there is any doubt. A label should be placed on the cup lid with pertinent information such as morph, sex, and birthdate.

Temperatures and weather conditions should be monitored in advance of shipping at all points, including ship from and to cities as well as hubs in between. Geckos should never be shipped at times when there are storms or temperature extremes indicated in forecasts.

Careful tracking should be done for each shipment, and tracking numbers should be provided to the recipient so they can monitor the progress of their precious cargo.

If shipping temperatures are going to exceed $85^{\circ}F$, cold packs should be used to prevent overheating of the animal. A minimum of an 8 ounce ice pack should be used, and if the weather is very warm I prefer to use a 16 ounce cold pack. The extra weight in shipping is worth the cost to ensure the gecko arrives safely. Excessive heat can kill a gecko quickly. If using a cold pack, the geckos' deli cups should be placed on the bottom of the box, crumpled paper should be placed on the cups to insulate them from getting too cold, and then the cold pack should be placed on top and backfilled with paper.

Even though geckos need very little airflow, I always recommend punching a small hole on two sides of the box so the box isn't completely air tight. Seal the box with good quality clear packing tape, being careful not to cover the air holes.

I have done very critical studies using this method. I put the shipment together as described above during temperatures in the 90's for 24 hours. In place of a gecko I put a high quality LED digital thermometer probe in the deli cup, with the readout outside the box so I could monitor the temperatures over a 24 hour period in extreme heat conditions. I packed the cup as described along with a 16 ounce shipping ice pack. The last two hours of the 24 hour period, I placed the box in a car with the windows up. Temperatures inside the vehicle got up to $125^{\circ}F$. The readout temperature of the box never got above $85^{\circ}F$, which proved to me that this method was safe even in extreme heat conditions. Again, it is well-advised to use a 16 ounce cold pack in these conditions, and ideally, not even take the chance of shipping animals under such hot conditions. It is always best to wait until temperatures moderate, but if it is necessary to ship animals in very warm conditions, following these guidelines will most likely result in a safe shipment. When in doubt, do not ship.

Conversely, I used the same study method to evaluate shipments in cold conditions. First of all, I never use shipping heat packs of less duration than 60-72 hours. I still see many breeders using 24 or 40 hour heat packs, and in my experience it is a mistake and puts the animals in possible jeopardy due to frequent failures. I recall receiving a shipment of young animals some years back in cold conditions that were sent with one 40 hour heat pack taped to the lid. All of the geckos had necrotic, frost bitten tails...very tragic.

The 60-72 hour heat packs are very reliable and provide a significant amount of warmth for a longer period of time. Also, in the event of a plane cancellation, malfunction, or any sort of delay, the longer duration heat pack gives you a bigger window of shipping safety.

When using heat packs, taping the heat pack to the lid does virtually nothing to keep the animals below warm based on my studies. Place heat packs on the bottom of the box (heat rises), insulate the pack from the deli cups with some crumpled paper so the geckos don't get overheated, and backfill the box with more paper for insulation and shock absorption.

Under extreme cold conditions, our similar studies in cold weather proved that our method worked well and the interior of the box stayed in a normal range. It is also a good idea when shipping in cold weather to have the box held at the local courier hub for pickup. That will avoid a few hours of the geckos bouncing around in a cold delivery truck.

While many of these guidelines are simple common sense, it is amazing how many stories I hear where people did not use good shipping practices, often with tragic results. As I said, when in doubt, do not ship. You, the recipient, and the geckos will greatly appreciate your patience and diligence.

As far as receiving geckos, there are some dos and don'ts. When first receiving the box, place it in a quiet safe location for a period of 20-30 minutes so the gecko can settle down after a long and arduous journey. Then, open the box quietly and carefully, speaking in soft reassuring tones as you unbox the new arrivals. Remember that the little creatures have been through a lot in the previous 24 hours, so they need to feel safe and comfortable.

When you unbox them, hold them very briefly to reassure them all is OK, and place them into their new enclosure, which should have been set up properly in advance of their arrival. Leave them alone for a couple days, being sure to just provide them with fresh water and mealworms and monitor them minimally to be sure they are OK and not shedding, etc.

After a couple days, you can attempt to handle them very briefly to show them all is OK, but don't overdo it. Once you see some mealworms starting to disappear, you know the gecko is acclimating and you can begin to interact with it for brief periods.

If you have existing animals, new arrivals should be quarantined from the other geckos until you are sure that their health is good. Observe new arrivals carefully. Always handle new arrivals last when working with your gecko group.

It is also advisable to take a fresh fecal sample to your vet for analysis to ensure you are not introducing a possible pathogen into your collection. Many breeders do routine parasite screening of their colonies, so it is always advisable to obtain geckos from reliable sources. This is a good question to ask when purchasing any kind of animal. If the breeder acts puzzled about your question, it may be a good idea to find another supplier. Most breeders however are ethical and undoubtedly do some sort of health monitoring of their colonies. Having said that, it is still a good idea to have an initial fecal sample analyzed, as well as routine analysis of your colony to confirm that your animals are parasite-free.

There are many good resources available on shipping and receiving practices for reptiles, and it is a good idea to educate yourself on this crucial aspect so you can avoid problems down the road.

CHAPTER 13

Emergency Preparedness

Al responsible pet owners should take emergency preparedness very seriously, and have a plan in place in case some sort of event were to occur that could potentially put our animals that are in our care in potential jeopardy. These disaster events often occur without warning, and scrambling at the last minute can have catastrophic effects on our beloved animals.

Having been through a major power outage for several days myself after a severe ice storm, I was glad that I had preparations in place, and my geckos survived and did just fine because I was prepared. Remember that our pets rely on our care and safety assurance…they can't take care of themselves. We owe it to them to be prepared, and this process is really quite simple.

Everyone should have a stockpile of 72 hour heat packs in their storage locker or somewhere in a secure, dry place that is easily accessible in the event of an emergency. Placing a 72 hour heat pack on every warm hide will ensure that your geckos will have enough warmth in the event of a furnace malfunction or power outage. This a minimal investment and may make the difference in whether your geckos survive or not. Buying heat packs from a reputable company is essential so you know that they are not old and outdated and will function properly when you need them. Do NOT use 24 or 40 hour heat packs as they have a high failure rate and even when they do work properly, they do not afford adequate heat in the event that your house temperature plummets to

50^0F or below. You should have at least two heat packs for each gecko cave, so that will give you a 6 day window in case of a prolonged power outage.

Another adjunct to this is to purchase a propane heater that runs on small propane torch tanks. You can purchase a very good quality propane heater for less than $50, and they are actually quite safe and efficient, and provide considerable heat to a room. Also, buy several small propane tanks and store them in a safe location. During a power outage, everyone is running to the stores in the area to buy propane heaters and tanks, so don't wait till an event happens to try to buy these items.

An excellent investment for the serious collector is a portable gasoline generator. You can operate this outdoors and run an extension cord into your reptile room to power an electric heater for many hours until your power returns. While a good generator can costs hundreds of dollars, it is money well spent and will give you peace of mind that you will have power no matter what happens.

The best investment is a natural gas generator that can power your home indefinitely. This is a must for large scale breeding operations, and an extremely good investment for the serious hobbyist with a valuable collection. A high quality, whole house generator will cost up to $5000, but is a great investment, will power your entire house or reptile building, and increases the value of your property considerably. This type of generator needs to be installed by a licensed electrician, and it must have a transfer switch to prevent power from feeding back through the power lines and putting power company workers in jeopardy.

A gas generator is the ultimate solution, and can keep your entire property operational no matter what type of power outage or catastrophe should occur, as long as there is natural gas available of course. The added benefit of this type of generator is that it also keeps your property cool in the event of a hot weather power outage when you need to have cooling operational.

While geckos can go for extended periods of time without food, it is always good to have adequate supplies of mealworms on hand so if there is some sort of event, you will have food for your valuable geckos, especially for young geckos that need to eat daily. You should also purchase several gallons of water and put them in nearby storage. If the bottles are sealed, water lasts indefinitely, and while geckos can go without food for a while, they must always have access to water since dehydration can quickly put geckos in jeopardy.

It is also wise to have neighbors or friends who live close by be fully trained in caring for your animals. In the event of an emergency, you could be stranded for a considerable time, and it is essential to have backup that you can rely on in the event you can't get home for an extended period of time.

Finally, while we all hope to live forever, sometimes things happen. Since geckos live for many years, it is good to think about someone you can rely on to take over your collection if something were to incapacitate you for a long period of time. It is wise to put your gecko collection in your will as well. While it's very rare, we've heard of a few male leopard geckos living into their 30s, so you need to take this into account in your planning process.

These are some of the key items to take into account. The bottom line is to sit down and make a plan. Once you've addressed these issues, you'll sleep better knowing that no matter what, your beloved little friends will be taken care of properly. And always remember that Murphy's Law axiom.

CHAPTER 14

Products and Sources

As stated before, whether you are obtaining geckos or supplies and equipment, it is important to always think of quality as the number one priority. The old adage, you get what you pay for holds true, particularly if you plan to grow in the hobby from hobbyist, to collector, and perhaps even to breeder. With this in mind, finding the vendors and companies that can best fill those needs for your pursuits is something that requires time and effort, as well as networking. Speaking with those who have been successful in the leopard gecko arena is a great way to find out the right sources for your needs.

We are fortunate that there are many excellent companies and individuals who are dedicated to quality supplies and equipment to help us as we move forward in the field. The explosion of information online has revolutionized the reptile field as it has all facets of our lives these days. There is an enormous amount of information online, and spending time perusing these internet resources will be of tremendous help, as is networking with gecko people on the online forums and at reptile shows.

The same holds true with obtaining geckos. There are many excellent suppliers who can help you to find the geckos of your choosing. I've found that contacting various reputable breeders is a great way to find who has what morph that you may be looking for, as well as who can provide you with the best service. When I first entered the gecko field, I quickly found out the helpful sources, and also those who were too busy to answer my questions and provide assistance. The good suppliers are golden, and are successful because of their caring for both the geckos and the hobbyists.

I spent a great deal of time and funds to travel around the U.S. to meet some of the breeders I chose to do business with, and they were most gracious in spending time with me, showing me their operations, and helping to put me on the right path. Their dedication was most inspiring to me, and I value them greatly as colleagues and friends to this day.

While they may not have time to meet with every individual, they will most certainly interact with everyone in a professional and courteous manner whether online, via phone, or at reptile shows, and will provide invaluable service and advice.

As for suppliers of feeder insects, there are many companies, big and small, who will be able to provide you with quality insects and great service. These relationships are crucial, especially if you choose to develop a collection and perhaps breed geckos. If for some reason you suddenly are in need of insects for your geckos, you need suppliers that are willing to go the extra mile to take prompt action to get you what you need, and at a reasonable price.

If you do produce geckos for sale, you will need to align yourself with a reliable courier that will safely and efficiently transport your geckos to their destination. To be a certified reptile shipper, you will often need to go through a process to be allowed to use that courier's service, and you must follow their guidelines carefully to achieve certification.

Costs of shipping can vary widely, so you need to take costs into careful consideration so you can ship animals in a competitive, cost effective way if you endeavor to sell and ship geckos. There are also services that will ship your animals for you by using their online services for your shipping order and print out of your shipping labels. For many smaller breeders, this is an excellent service that can provide good group pricing since they deal with numerous breeders and get larger shipping price discounts from the couriers. International shipments are a bit more difficult to coordinate, but there are services that will ship your geckos internationally, though the cost is often prohibitive for the average breeder.

Equipment and supplies are best obtained from online sources to get the best pricing. The large reptile equipment companies generally will not sell directly to individuals, so you will need to go through distributors and stores to obtain products from them. They usually have stringent requirements, and you generally must have a storefront operation to be able to purchase wholesale through the large manufacturers and suppliers.

As for rack systems, do your research carefully, and talk to others in the field to find what equipment is best for your particular application and space constraints. I have found that the racks that have more of a closed design generally provide much better temperature stability from top to bottom, and are the most energy efficient.

Remember to use good quality proportional thermostats to regulate rack systems in order to keep your temperatures in a tight range. Keep in mind that the best rack suppliers are often very busy, so give yourself a couple months lead time to ensure your racks will be built and shipped to you in time for when you need to put them into use.

Last but not least, always follow good care procedures and use high quality water, vitamins, and supplements. Bottled spring water is best for obvious reasons, so find a good source for your water. Be sure you use vitamins/supplements from a well-known company that provides a full ingredient analysis, and always check expiration dates so you don't use possible outdated lots.

Your suppliers are an important part of your team, so select them wisely. They will be an immense help as you move forward in your aspirations to become the next great reptile operation.

Finding quality vendors that can provide the equipment and supplies for your operation is a high priority, whether you just have one gecko, or a store full. They will also be valuable resources of information for you as you grow in the hobby.

CHAPTER 15

Gecko Health Care

O ne of the great attributes of leopard geckos as pets is the very low cost of health care. You generally don't need to worry about infectious or zoonotic disease concerns, exorbitant vet bills, routine vaccinations, high premiums and deductibles, or malfunctioning websites. Leopard geckos have evolved through time to be very hardy and resilient little animals. Originating from the very rugged environments of the Middle East where they have to survive difficult conditions, extremes in temperature and humidity, periods of very minimal food and water, etc., these are very tough critters that have few health issues under the ideal conditions that hobbyists now raise them in.

That being said, I will touch on a few of the more common maladies that can affect leopard geckos. Please be advised that while most health issues that arise are generally very minor in nature, an experienced reptile veterinarian should be consulted immediately if there is ever any doubt about the well-being of your gecko. The old adage, "if you can't afford the vet, don't get the pet" holds true with leopard geckos as with any animal. Animals depend on us for their proper care, and as good guardians of these wonderful creatures, we owe it to them to always be sure that they are cared for properly, in sickness and in health.

Shedding issues – The most common health issue with leopard geckos is incomplete shedding. Leopard geckos shed their skin routinely. Experienced gecko keepers know to look for the preliminary stage of shedding, which is a cloudy skin appearance. Moisture must be placed in the gecko's hides at the first onset of this cloudy skin. This can be easily accomplished by placing a piece of paper towel, crumpled and wet, inside each hide to add humidity to the caves, facilitating shedding.

Inexperienced gecko keepers, hobbyists who do not check their geckos at least once a day, breeders, and collectors who have large colonies and cannot monitor their geckos pre-shed stage routinely, should use moist hides at all times. Moist hides are also a good idea for white geckos and very light albinos because it can be difficult to ascertain the pre-shed stage in these geckos.

For experienced keepers and those who monitor their geckos at least daily, it is unnecessary to utilize a moist hide 24/7, as long as moisture is added at the pre-shed stage. As discussed previously, I generally do not recommend humid hides for reasons that I mentioned in that chapter.

After a gecko has shed, the gecko must be taken out into good light and thoroughly examined for possible shed remnants, with particular concentration of areas such as the eyelids, jawline, legs, toes, and vent region. Shed remnants left on the eyelid area can cause serious and permanent injury to the eyes, and remnants on the toes will quickly (within hours), constrict the capillaries of the toes, causing necrosis and possibly even toe loss, which is permanent.

If the gecko has remnants of shed, more than just a few particles that can be easily removed with a warm, wet Q-tip, then soaking is in order. Fill a bowl with about an inch of warm water (depending on the size of the gecko), and soak the gecko in the warm bath for 5-10 minutes. Swab the affected areas of the face, back, or tail with paper towel soaked in the warm water. Then carefully remove all shed remnants.

If there are any raw or injured areas, apply a small amount of an antibiotic ointment to the area to prevent possible infection, and maintain scrupulous hygiene in the animal's enclosure to prevent infection. Necrotic toes can heal if caught early enough.

As with any health issue, prevention is always the best solution, so following good care aspects will go a long way in avoiding these shedding issues.

Skin, eye, and respiratory infections – Leopard geckos rarely get skin infections, but they can happen. Again, good hygiene and high quality care normally prevents these types of issues. Abrasions can happen, and often times skin injuries can occur during the mating process. At the first sign of an open wound or abrasion, gently clean the area and apply a small amount of antibiotic ointment with a Q-tip. Observe the area daily to be sure it is healing properly. Leopard geckos are very fast healers, so if this does not resolve quickly, it may be advisable to make an appointment with your veterinarian to see if antibiotic intervention may be warranted.

The same holds true with eye infections...at the first sign of inflammation or a wet or crusty discharge, often times a small amount of antibiotic ointment can resolve the problem. If it hasn't resolved quickly however, a trip to the vet is in order, as permanent eye injury can happen quickly.

Respiratory infections are rare, but at the first signs of sneezing, labored breathing, or any oral mucous discharge, it's time to see the vet. Often times, oral administration of a broad spectrum antibiotic like Baytril can resolve the problem in a few days.

Following proper care and husbandry practices will avoid many of these infection-type issues. Adhere to good hygienic animal care with clean substrate, maintain temperatures in the prescribed range, provide a high quality diet with proper supplementation, and you will find leopard geckos to be a very trouble-free and low cost animal to keep.

Stomatitis - This disease of the mouth area sometimes known as mouth rot, can occur from injury or an abscess. (I always recommend using blunt tipped forceps for feeding geckos to avoid injury to the mouth from sharp forceps.) Geckos can get a small crusty area in the gum region, accompanied by swelling and inflammation. This can quickly progress to a serious issue if not addressed promptly and thoroughly. The area should be carefully and gently swabbed with a folded piece of gauze soaked in a dilute Betadine or Nolvasan solution three to four times a day to disinfect the area and remove the debris.

Mouth rot can be very problematic and should be examined by a veterinarian if the problem does not resolve in few days. If caught early however, this generally has a good result, though it may leave some scarring to the mouth area that was affected.

Metabolic Bone Disease - One of the most serious and debilitating diseases leopard geckos can be afflicted by is MBD or metabolic bone disease. The good news again is that this disease is 100% preventable. Geckos, as with all animals, need adequate supplies of calcium for many health processes. If calcium blood levels are low, calcium can be leached from the geckos' bones, causing the bones to become soft and the joints to quickly deteriorate. The gecko then can no longer eat, stand, or walk normally and its health can decline very rapidly.

Young geckos must have their insects lightly dusted with calcium plus D3, mixed with a good quality reptile vitamin preparation. This will ensure that they have adequate levels of calcium and vital minerals to allow for proper bone growth. Once the gecko has reached the size of 25-30 grams, the insects generally do not need to be dusted (older geckos prefer their insects not be dusted), however a shallow dish of vitamins and calcium with D3 should be provided in their enclosure at all times, and they will lap up this mixture as they intuitively know they need more supplements. It is also necessary to be sure the calcium preparation has D3 in it, as D3 is an essential hormone that promotes proper assimilation of calcium.

If a gecko does get MBD, it is crucial to take prompt action. If it is in the very early stages of MBD, you can make a suspension in water of the calcium D3 and vitamin supplements and carefully administer the suspension orally once a day. If the gecko also is not eating, then the suspension should also contain food as described previously. If the MBD does not start to improve immediately, it is essential to take the animal to a reptile vet for possible administration of injectable calcium.

As they say, an ounce of prevention is worth a pound of cure, so please be sure you follow these guidelines and MBD will be an acronym you'll never have to worry about in your gecko care program.

Impaction - Geckos intestines are very small and can become impacted if they ingest substrate material such as sand or other particulate matter. Never use live plants in your terrarium setup, as the gecko can ingest soil which not only can harbor possible pathogens, but can impact the animal. Sand should never be used as a substrate for this reason. If impaction is suspected, feeding waxworms for a few days will provide extra fat in the diet that may help the animal pass its stool.

If the impaction does not resolve, veterinary intervention should be considered promptly. Parasite evaluation should be done as well to rule out possible parasite infection.

Parasitic infections - Luckily, pathogenic parasites are generally not a problem with most gecko colonies. Good breeding operations perform routine parasite screening and many treat their colonies prophylactically to ensure their colonies are free of parasites. Hobbyists should also have periodic parasite screening done at their vet clinic. A simple fecal flotation is often adequate, is inexpensive to perform, and will identify most common reptile parasites such as pinworms.

Common parasites can usually be eliminated easily with Panacur dosing orally. This is an anthelmintic drug that eradicates many common parasites quite effectively. It must be obtained through a veterinarian who will dilute the medication to the appropriate dosage for leopard geckos. Panacur is a very safe drug if used according to directions. Overdosage/toxicity is extremely rare, and it is administered orally via syringe in very low doses. It is often dosed twice, one week apart. There is a recent school of thought that indicates that three consecutive doses (daily for three days) is also very effective, and is now preferred by some veterinarians.

When taking a fecal sample to your vet for parasite testing, the sample must be as fresh as possible, and can be refrigerated for a short time if need be until you can get it to your vet clinic. I recommend an annual fecal test be run for most hobbyists to assure that your gecko did not pick something up along the way. All new geckos coming into a colony should be quarantined and tested to be sure you are not introducing a parasite into your colony.

There are other parasitic infections that can be very difficult to eradicate such as Cryptosporidium, a protozoan parasite that is highly infectious and most often, lethal. Always obtain geckos from good breeding sources that adhere to a good care program, and the chances of your gecko being infected with a pathogenic organism like "crypto" will be great reduced.

Tail loss - Nothing can be more traumatic to a gecko, and its owner, than a dropped tail. Fortunately, it is a rare event, and something the average hobbyist will never encounter. Causes of tail loss are cage mate aggression (another reason that individual housing is optimal), aggression during breeding (usually avoided if you use the individual breeding method rather than colony breeding), sudden trauma such as dropping your gecko when handling improperly, loud sudden noise like a loud barking dog, illness, improper care techniques, and extreme fear. Barking dogs can be particularly alarming to a gecko, and care should be taken to avoid placing enclosures near areas where geckos can be subjected to loud barking.

A dropped tail is often not particularly difficult to treat, and the tail will regenerate to a certain extent, but it certainly will never look as nice as the original tail. Females who have dropped tails can still be bred in the future, and geckos that lose tails can heal and live a normal life. Occasionally however, tail loss can be so traumatic that the gecko can expire, so it is best to prevent this from happening by being cognizant of the causes and taking care to avoid putting geckos in harm's way so the event doesn't happen. If your gecko does drop its tail, it is best to leave the gecko alone for a day or two to allow it to recover from the trauma of the event and for the tail stub to clot and dry. Once it is dry and the gecko is stable, you can apply a small amount of antibiotic ointment to the injury to prevent infection and promote healing.

Summary – These are a few of the more common health issues one can encounter with leopard geckos. Others, such as egg binding, severe infections, debilitating MBD, wasting, and other serious afflictions require prompt intervention by a veterinarian. Remember, our geckos rely on us for their well-being, so following a good care program will go a long way in preventing health issues that can be traumatic for your gecko, and you.

CHAPTER 16

The Hobby and the Business

Many people who get a leopard gecko consider breeding geckos because they become so excited about just how wonderful these animals really are. They soon think about starting breeding projects of their own, initially perhaps to add to their own collection or to provide them to friends and family. This often evolves into thoughts of starting their own little side business to generate income. During difficult economic times, this may seem like a great idea to pay their bills and work for yourself, but in actuality, tough economic times are the worst times to attempt to start a new business venture of any kind, no less trying to sell animals to a public that may not have much disposable income at the time. Nonetheless, many decide to take the plunge and endeavor to try their hands at breeding geckos and become the next hot breeder in the gecko world.

I have witnessed this many times, where people will buy a couple leopard geckos, get excited, and before you know it they are ordering racks, equipment, and many geckos from various breeders. I recall one individual who flew out to our Colorado store and purchased a group of geckos, saying he was going to dabble in the business on a small scale to see what he could develop. Soon after, he was buying groups of geckos from many breeders, ordering rack systems, building a website, and the plunge was on... A year later, he contacted me to tell me he was in over his head, couldn't sell his offspring the way he had hoped, and asked me if I was interested in buying his collection, at a major financial loss to him. This story occurs far too often in the reptile business, and it is sad for the budding entrepreneur as well for the geckos who they need to find homes for.

When we decided to open the first commercial leopard gecko storefront in the world, many established reptile breeders said we were crazy! Not only was the economy extremely poor at the time, but being pioneers of sorts and diving into uncharted waters seemed ludicrous to most everyone we talked to.

When we were on the fence as to whether or not to proceed, we met with the planning boards of the local communities to get their approval and input, and they were overwhelming positive about our business plan. I recall speaking with the head of the planning board for our hometown, and he said that he had reviewed many business plans through the years, and that he felt strongly that our business would succeed.

Our local county also had to review and permit our new store operation. I remember being on vacation in Hawaii at the time of their decision. I recall laying on the beach in Maui, when my cell phone rang...ah yes, the days of technology! The person on the other end was in charge of reviewing our business plan. She said they had just convened a meeting of the county planning board where they reviewed our business plan, and even put our online business website up on the conference room screen for all to see and review. She said that they unanimously approved our business, and added that everyone was very excited about our new venture. These positive responses gave us the added impetus we needed to move forward with our plan to start up the first and only gecko store in the world, and the rest is history.

Designer Geckos Store. The first commercial storefront in the world was originally founded in Longmont, Colorado. One of the primary focuses of the store continues to be on education, and it hosts school field trips from the surrounding areas and trains interns on leopard gecko biology and care.

The reptile business is a very difficult one to break into. Many have tried, and unfortunately failed. There are many very established breeders in the field who have the knowledge, infrastructure, staff, and know how to maintain their businesses, even in a difficult economy. So how is a new kid on the block going to be one of the survivors? Statistically, it takes 2-3 years for new businesses to show a profit, so it is important to keep this in mind.

Well, all is not gloom and doom. Many do succeed, even if only on a small scale. There are keys to this success, and proper planning is of paramount importance. I always first ask people considering this as a business if they are willing to work seven days a week, including nights, weekends, and holidays. Geckos need daily care, particularly babies, and there must be a 100% commitment or it simply will not work out. I also advise people to have a support network in place of other like-minded, dedicated people who are willing to make this sacrifice of time and effort. That is a tall order in today's world where everyone is so busy and life is hectic.

The people I know who have succeeded have a very dedicated staff, partner, spouse, friends, or manager that they can rely on heavily to support the business and maintain high levels of quality, care, and customer service. There will invariably be times when you just cannot be available for the geckos, such as illness, business, family obligations, and even vacation (which often are few and far between for reptile breeders). This support aspect cannot be overstated.

I also feel that committing to high quality animals, an outstanding care program, and excellent customer service are keys. Pet quality geckos are wonderful and will always be in need in the reptile community, but keep in mind that it costs just as much to produce, grow, and maintain a $15 gecko as it does a $400 gecko. There is a lot of work involved in raising animals from hatchlings, and the cost of labor, food, and overhead must be considered if you are to make a profit. Sticking to high quality geckos with known genetics and health profiles will go a long way in getting you on the road to success. This also allows you to produce a smaller number of animals, keep your workload manageable, your costs down, and your staffing needs minimal. Even in a bad economy, there are individuals who have the funds to buy geckos, but their focus is most often on high quality animals.

Keeping it simple is important, and specializing in a few projects to get your feet wet will allow you to assess your business and grow it accordingly. Also concentrate on excellent equipment and rack systems. Remember that maintaining stable temperatures are one of the most important elements in producing high quality geckos. Generally with rack systems, you get what you pay for, and this is no aspect to try to cut your spending. Quality racks are well designed and keep temperatures much more stable than most homemade racks or inexpensive setups.

Thermostats should be of high quality, and diligent temperature monitoring is critical. Also, align yourself with good feeder insect vendors.

It is important to have good relationships with all your vendors, particularly your insect suppliers. They take care of their regular customers, and in a pinch during times of critical need, they will take care of you. Also, having a good website is important since many will likely find out about you online and may want to purchase animals from you through your website. Having solid customer service procedures in place, and knowing how to ship animals properly is a must. There are services that can assist you in shipping your animals. Shipping on your own through the large carriers requires you to have a viable business and be certified, which may be difficult for someone just starting out.

Another crucial element is to have a market for your animals. Many start to breed animals without thoroughly thinking through how they plan to sell them. This should be one of the very first considerations when delving into this whole idea of breeding geckos. There are many established, experienced breeders already set up and doing business with strong reputations, so you need to consider whether your geckos will be marketable and how you will endeavor to sell them.

I don't mean to make starting a gecko business sound like a daunting task, but it is important for you to know what is involved and not something to take a cavalier approach about. Geckos are wonderful animals, but they rely on us as their guardians to be properly schooled and to keep their well-being and safety as our number one priority. If you take all these elements into account, and feel that you can provide a 100% commitment, then this business just may be for you.

Now, breeding geckos and owning your own small business may be the right fit for some, but for others, having a gecko or two may be all they really wish to do. This is actually an enviable pursuit, and I'm sure many breeders working long hours must sometimes fantasize about how nice it would be to just have a few geckos that they can give all their care and attention to.

As I've stated previously, the more time and effort you can spend with individual geckos, the more you can socialize them and develop their intelligence and personality. Having one or just a few geckos allows you to spend considerable time with them, and you'll be amazed at the results. Conversely, having large numbers of geckos permits very little time to spend quality time with your favorites. I still try to give as much time as I can to my most coveted geckos, and have developed them to levels that have astounded me. I often think what they might be like if I could give them hours of my time instead of minutes, and this is a sacrifice that we breeders make to provide geckos to others.

Whatever direction you choose to take in this great field, be sure you give it significant thought and don't make decisions based on emotions, but rather on practicality and realism.

CHAPTER 17

Care Summary

We have gone into considerable depth in the preceding chapters regarding leopard gecko care, and hopefully you've found this information to be useful as you progress in the leopard gecko hobby, whether you are a novice or an experienced keeper. While some of my methods can be deemed as far different from the prevailing wisdom on gecko care, these methods have proven to be very successful in producing high quality geckos. I encourage everyone to take the time to learn all you can about these fascinating animals that I believe are like none other.

I routinely field questions from around the world from hobbyists who have questions or concerns about their geckos, whether they are a customer of ours or not. I will continue to try to be a resource as well as an advocate for the proper and humane care of leopard geckos, and encourage all experienced hobbyists and breeders to do the same. There is still a lot of erroneous information out there on leopard gecko care, and our goal needs to be to educate and improve on this so everyone can enjoy this great hobby to the fullest, and that the geckos we covet will have happy and healthy lives.

As previously stated, I encourage gecko hobbyists to get involved in educational aspects of the hobby, attend and even give seminars, attend reptile shows in your area, and try to assist reptile rescue operations by donating your time or funds.

As you get more and more involved in the leopard gecko hobby, you realize just how special these wonderful creatures really are. I think the hobby will continue to grow and flourish, and amazing new morphs will continue to be discovered by breeding experts and budding gecko scientists alike. I see the day when many of the stunning morphs of today will be produced in super giant sizes, and that there will be new variations created that will be astounding.

I thank you all for your interest in leopard geckos, and for the passion and zeal I have witnessed through the years by those involved in this great field.

Having been associated with many groups of people in my life, including major pharmaceutical organizations, professional sports, media, and professional music, I've found reptile enthusiasts to be some of the most admirable and dedicated people I've ever been involved with, and my life has been enriched because of them…and of course…the geckos!

Black Night. These spectacular black geckos will someday come in many different crosses and sizes. Someone will perhaps produce a Black Night Super Giant...could be you...

Why Leopard Geckos are the #1 Reptile Pet

- They are very friendly and easy to tame...they love people
- They are very clean animals, with no odors, and can be paper trained
- They are hypo-allergenic, perfect for children & people with allergies
- They come in many beautiful colors and patterns
- They can be left alone when you are away on vacation
- Adults eat very little so they are very low maintenance
- They are nocturnal, sleep during the day, and ready to play at night
- They are inexpensive to feed and keep
- They are the perfect pet, a beautiful living toy for all ages
- Males live 10-20 years, females 10-12 on average
- They can be taken anywhere when the weather is warm
- They love TV and can sit with you on the couch!

Mealworm Care and Feeding

Mealworms are an excellent food for geckos. They are high in nutrition, but also need to be fed and cared for. When you feed mealworms to your gecko, they need to be properly "gutloaded" so they are very nourishing to the gecko.

Please follow these instructions to keep your mealworms healthy:

Mealworms must be refrigerated so they do not turn into pupae and beetles. When you refrigerate your mealworms, be sure you do not place the container in the super cold zone of the refrigerator. Also, be sure you have airholes in the container so the mealworms can breathe. A small tupperware container with holes in the top works very well. Use organic oat bran as the bedding for your mealworms in the fridge.

Every two weeks, take the container out of the fridge, sprinkle a thin layer of insect food on the surface, and place some fresh organic carrots sliced lengthwise in with the mealworms. Leave this container out at room temperature for 24 hours so the mealworms can eat. After 24 hours, remove the carrots and place the container back into the fridge. This will keep your mealworms fed and healthy for months.

Every 3-4 days, take out as many mealworms as you'll need to feed your geckos for that period of time, place them in a small bowl, put in some insect food and fresh organic carrot slices, and leave that dish at room temp....these gutloaded mealworms are what you will feed to your gecko. For young geckos under 30 grams, be sure to put a pinch of your mineral/vitamin mixture in the mealworm dish so your growing gecko gets enough of those important supplements.

Also discard any black or dried out mealworms. If any mealworms turn into white pupae, discard those as well since the gecko will not eat them.

Suppliers and Sources

Designer Geckos uses various vendors for its supplies and equipment, and we thank them for their service. The following are some of the suppliers we use and have had great success with, but these are not exclusive endorsements. We encourage everyone to find the suppliers that work best for your applications.

Terrariums and accessories sold through distributors and stores:

Exo Terra – high quality terrariums and accessories: www.exo-terra.com

Zoo Med – excellent accessories, heat pads, thermostats: www.zoomed.com

Zilla – reptile carpet liners and other accessories: www.zilla-rules.com

Rep Cal – high quality calcium supplements and vitamins: www.repcal.com

Feeder insects sold online by these outlets:

Bugco – mealworms, waxworms, superworms: www.ebugco.com

Grubco – mealworms, waxworms, superworms: www.grubco.com

Mulberry Farms – silkworms, hornworms, etc.: www.mulberryfarms.com

Precut paper supplier:

Shepherd Specialty Papers – www.ssponline.com

Germicidal disinfectant:

Pharmacal Research Labs – www.pharmacal.com

Picture Gallery

The following are some recent pictures of the Designer Geckos collection and geckos we have produced as examples of the types of geckos we have been working on. The combinations, crosses, and new morphs that will be produced in the future by hobbyists, collectors, and breeders worldwide will be astounding.

Banded Lavender Designer and Reverse Striped Snow Eclipse

Mack Super Snow

Tangerine Bandit

Striped Hot Moose Super Giant

Bold Stripe Mack Snow

Sunglow Super Giant Juvenile

Light Phase Mack Snow Juvenile

Mandarin Tangerine

Black and White Bandit Juvenile

Firefox Juvenile

Very unique Buffalo Bill Mack Snow Juvenile

Zorro Mandarin Designer Juveniles

Zorro Bandit

Firefox Juvenile

Zorro Bandit Juvenile

Super Bold Zorro Bandit Juvenile

Buffalo Bill Giant Mack Snow Juvenile

Hot Moose Raptor Super Giant

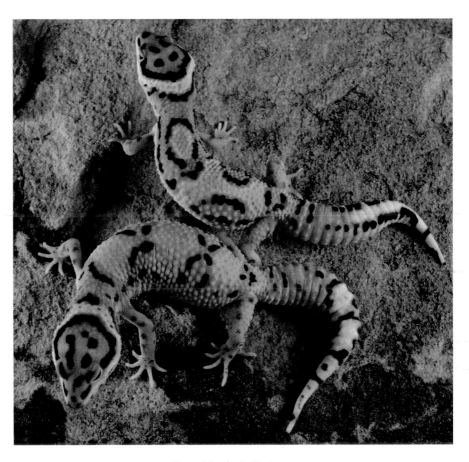

Zorro Mandarin Designers

Zorro Bandit

Hot Moose Super Giant

Mandarin Tangerine Enigma Giant

Firefox Designer

Tremper Albino Super Giant

White and Yellow

Zorro Mandarin Designer

Mandarin Tangerine Enigma Juveniles. These little sisters show why many of us have gotten so enthralled with the leopard gecko hobby.

Black Nights. One of the most important aspects of any reptile business is to keep up with the latest developments in new morphs that are up and coming. These Black Nights, (produced by breeder Ferry Zuurmond and facilitated by Roy Sluiter), a new morph 15 years in the making, are now part of Designer Geckos' extensive breeding collection. This incredibly beautiful new morph will be offered to the gecko community in the near future. Not only is this a stunning morph, but the cross possibilities are endless and will undoubtedly produce some of the most beautiful geckos in the history of the hobby.

Seeing the joy in gecko hobbyists' faces is what it's all about. The educational aspects of
the hobby, as well as the companionship of these wonderful animals will continue to
make leopard geckos one of the most popular and exciting pets
in the world for many years to come.

Conclusion

Thank you for your interest in this book. Hopefully, you have found it to be a useful tool for you as you move forward in your pursuits of this wonderful hobby.

Best wishes to you, and I hope you have a wonderful and rewarding experience with the best little animals on the planet. I'm sure you will!